PENPALS
for
Handwriting

Year 4 Teacher's Book
(8–9 years)

Gill Budgell   Kate Ruttle

Series Consultants
Sue Palmer   Professor Rhona Stainthorp

Contents

CAMBRIDGE **HITACHI**

www.cambridge-hitachi.com

Scope and sequence

Foundation 1 / 3–5 years

DEVELOPING GROSS MOTOR SKILLS
1 The vocabulary of movement
2 Large movements
3 Responding to music

DEVELOPING FINE MOTOR SKILLS
4 Hand and finger play 6 Links to art
5 Making and modelling 7 Using one-handed tools and equipment

DEVELOPING PATTERNS AND BASIC LETTER MOVEMENTS
8 Pattern-making 12 Investigating circles
9 Responding to music 13 Investigating angled patterns
10 Investigating straight line patterns 14 Investigating eights and spirals
11 Investigating loops

Foundation 2 / Primary 1

Term 2
1 Introducing long ladder letters: *l, i, t, u, j, y*
2 Practising long ladder letters: *l, i*
3 Practising long ladder letters: *t, u*
4 Practising long ladder letters: *j, y*
5 Practising all the long ladder letters
6 Introducing one-armed robot letters: *r, b, n, h, m, k, p*
7 Practising one-armed robot letters: *b, n*
8 Practising one-armed robot letters: *h, m*
9 Practising one-armed robot letters: *k, p*
10 Practising all the one-armed robot letters
11 Introducing capitals for one-armed robot letters: *R, B, N, H, M, K, P*
12 Introducing capitals for long ladder letters: *L, I, T, U, J, Y*

Term 3
13 Introducing curly caterpillar letters: *c, a, d, o, s, g, q, e, f*
14 Practising curly caterpillar letters: *a, d*
15 Practising curly caterpillar letters: *o, s*
16 Practising curly caterpillar letters: *g, q*
17 Practising curly caterpillar letters: *e, f*
18 Practising all the curly caterpillar letters
19 Introducing zig-zag monster letters: *z, v, w, x*
20 Practising zig-zag monster letters: *v, w, x*
21 Introducing capitals for curly caterpillar letters: *C, A, D, O, S, G, Q, E, F*
22 Introducing capitals for zig-zag monster letters: *Z, V, W, X*
23 Exploring *ch*, *th* and *sh*

Year 1 / Primary 2

Term 1
1 Letter formation practice: long ladder family
2 Letter formation practice: one-armed robot family
3 Letter formation practice: curly caterpillar family
4 Letter formation practice: zig-zag monster family
5 Practising the vowels: *i*
6 Practising the vowels: *u*
7 Practising the vowels: *a*
8 Practising the vowels: *o*
9 Practising the vowels: *e*
10 Letter formation practice: capital letters

Term 2
11 Introducing diagonal join to ascender: joining *at, all*
12 Practising diagonal join to ascender: joining *th*
13 Practising diagonal join to ascender: joining *ch*
14 Practising diagonal join to ascender: joining *cl*
15 Introducing diagonal join, no ascender: joining *in, im*
16 Practising diagonal join, no ascender: joining *cr, tr, dr*
17 Practising diagonal join, no ascender: joining *lp, mp*
18 Introducing diagonal join, no ascender, to an anticlockwise letter: joining *id, ig*
19 Practising diagonal join, no ascender, to an anticlockwise letter: joining *nd, ld*
20 Practising diagonal join, no ascender, to an anticlockwise letter: joining *ng*

Term 3
21 Practising diagonal join, no ascender: joining *ee*
22 Practising diagonal join, no ascender: joining *ai, ay*
23 Practising diagonal join, no ascender: joining *ime, ine*
24 Introducing horizontal join, no ascender: joining *op, oy*
25 Practising horizontal join, no ascender: joining *one, ome*
26 Introducing horizontal join, no ascender, to an anticlockwise letter: joining *oa, og*
27 Practising horizontal join, no ascender, to an anticlockwise letter: joining *wa, wo*
28 Introducing horizontal join to ascender: joining *ol, ot*
29 Practising horizontal join to ascender: joining *wh, oh*
30 Introducing horizontal and diagonal joins to ascender, to an anticlockwise letter: joining *of, if*
31 Assessment

Year 2 / Primary 3

Term 1
1 How to join in a word: high-frequency words
2 Introducing the break letters: *j, g, x, y, z, b, f, p, q, r, s*
3 Practising diagonal join to ascender in words: *eel, eet*
4 Practising diagonal join, no ascender, in words: *a_e*
5 Practising diagonal join, no ascender, to an anticlockwise letter in words: *ice, ide*
6 Practising horizontal join, no ascender, in words: *ow, ou*
7 Practising horizontal join, no ascender, in words: *oy, oi*
8 Practising horizontal join, no ascender, to an anticlockwise letter in words: *oa, ode*
9 Practising horizontal join to ascender in words: *ole, obe*
10 Practising horizontal join to ascender in words: *ook, ool*

Term 2
11 Practising diagonal join to r: *ir, ur, er*
12 Practising horizontal join to r: *or, oor*
13 Introducing horizontal join from r to ascender: *url, irl, irt*
14 Introducing horizontal join from r: *ere*
15 Practising joining to and from r: *air*
16 Introducing diagonal join to s: *dis*
17 Introducing horizontal join to s: *ws*
18 Introducing diagonal join from s to ascender: *sh*
19 Introducing diagonal join from s, no ascender: *si, su, se, sp, sm*
20 Introducing horizontal join from r to an anticlockwise letter: *rs*

Term 3
21 Practising diagonal join to an anticlockwise letter: *ea, ear*
22 Introducing horizontal join to and from f to ascender: *ft, fl*
23 Introducing horizontal join from f, no ascender: *fu, fr*
24 Introducing *qu* (diagonal join, no ascender)
25 Introducing *rr* (horizontal join, no ascender)
26 Introducing *ss* (diagonal join, no ascender, to an anticlockwise letter)
27 Introducing *ff* (horizontal join to ascender)
28 Capital letter practice: height of ascenders and capitals
29 Assessment
30 Assessment

Scope and sequence

Year 3 / Primary 4

Term 1
1 Revising joins in a word: long vowel phonemes
2 Revising joins in a word: *le*
3 Revising joins in a word: *ing*
4 Revising joins in a word: high-frequency words
5 Revising joins in a word: new vocabulary
6 Revising joins in a word: *un*, *de*
7 Revising joins to and from s: *dis*
8 Revising joins to and from r: *re*, *pre*
9 Revising joins to and from f: *ff*
10 Revising joins: *qu*

Term 2
11 Introducing joining b and p: diagonal join, no ascender, *bi*, *bu*, *pi*, *pu*
12 Practising joining b and p: diagonal join, no ascender, to an anticlockwise letter, *ba*, *bo*, *pa*, *po*
13 Practising joining b and p: diagonal join to ascender, *bl*, *ph*
14 Relative sizes of letters: silent letters
15 Parallel ascenders: high-frequency words
16 Parallel descenders: adding *y* to words
17 Relative size and consistency: *ly*, *less*, *ful*
18 Relative size and consistency: capitals
19 Speed and fluency practice: *er*, *est*
20 Speed and fluency practice: opposites

Term 3
21 Consistency in spacing: *mis*, *anti*, *ex*
22 Consistency in spacing: *non*, *co*
23 Consistency in spacing: apostrophes
24 Layout, speed and fluency practice: address
25 Layout, speed and fluency practice: dialogue
26 Layout, speed and fluency practice: poem
27 Layout, speed and fluency practice: letter
28 Handwriting style
29 Assessment
30 Handwriting style

Year 4 / Primary 5

Term 1
1 Revising joins in a word: *ness*, *ship*
2 Revising joins in a word: *ing*, *ed*
3 Revising joins in a word: *s*
4 Revising joins in a word: *ify*
5 Revising joins in a word: *nn*, *mm*, *ss*
6 Revising parallel ascenders: *tt*, *ll*, *bb*
7 Revising parallel ascenders and descenders: *pp*, *ff*
8 Revising joins to an anticlockwise letter: *cc*, *dd*
9 Revising break letters: alphabetical order
10 Linking spelling and handwriting: related words

Term 2
11 Introducing sloped writing
12 Parallel ascenders: *al*, *ad*, *af*
13 Parallel descenders and break letters: *ight*, *ough*
14 Size, proportion and spacing: *ious*
15 Size, proportion and spacing: *able*, *ful*
16 Size, proportion and spacing: *fs*, *ves*
17 Speed and fluency: abbreviations for notes
18 Speed and fluency: notemaking
19 Speed and fluency: drafting
20 Speed and fluency: lists

Term 3
21 Size, proportion and spacing: *v*, *k*
22 Size, proportion and spacing: *ic*, *ist*
23 Size, proportion and spacing: *ion*
24 Size, proportion and spacing: contractions
25 Speed and fluency: *ible*, *able*
26 Speed and fluency: diminutives
27 Print alphabet
28 Print capitals
29 Assessment
30 Presentational skills: font styles

Years 5 & 6 / Primary 6 & 7

Year 5 Handwriting
1 Revision: practising sloped writing
2 Revision: practising the joins
3 Developing style for speed: joining from *t*
4 Developing style for speed: looping from *g*, *j* and *y*
5 Developing style for speed: joining from *f*
6 Developing style for speed: joining from *s*
7 Developing style for speed: writing *v*, *w*, *x* and *z* at speed
8 Developing style for speed: pen breaks in longer words
9 Different styles for different purposes
10 Assessment

Year 5 Project work
11 Haiku project: making notes
12 Haiku project: organising ideas
13 Haiku project: producing a draft
14 Haiku project: publishing the haiku
15 Haiku project: evaluation
16 Letter project: making notes
17 Letter project: structuring an argument
18 Letter project: producing a draft
19 Letter project: publishing a letter
20 Letter project: evaluation

Year 6 Handwriting
21 Self-assessment: evaluating handwriting
22 Self-assessment: checking the joins
23 Self-assessment: consistency of size
24 Self-assessment: letters resting on baseline
25 Self-assessment: ascenders and descenders
26 Self-assessment: consistency of size of capitals and ascenders
27 Writing at speed: inappropriate closing of letters
28 Writing at speed: identifying unclosed letters
29 Writing at speed: spacing within words
30 Writing at speed: spacing between words

Year 6 Project work
31 Playscript project: collecting information
32 Playscript project: recording ideas
33 Playscript project: producing a draft
34 Playscript project: publishing a playscript
35 Playscript project: evaluation
36 Information notice project: collecting and organising information
37 Information notice project: organising information
38 Information notice project: producing a draft
39 Information notice project: publishing a notice
40 Information notice project: evaluation

Even in this computer-literate age, good handwriting remains fundamental to our children's educational achievement. *Penpals for Handwriting* will help you teach children to develop fast, fluent, legible handwriting. The rationale for introducing joining is fully explained on page 11. This carefully structured handwriting scheme can also make a difference to overall attainment in writing.

Traditional principles in the contemporary classroom

We believe that:

1 A flexible, fluent and legible handwriting style empowers children to write with confidence and creativity. This is an entitlement that needs skilful teaching.

2 Handwriting is a developmental process with its own distinctive stages of sequential growth. We have identified five stages that form the basic organisational structure of *Penpals*:

  1 Readiness for handwriting; gross and fine motor skills leading to letter formation (Foundation / 3–5 years)

  2 Beginning to join (Key Stage 1 / 5–7 years)

  3 Securing the joins (Key Stage 1 and lower Key Stage 2 / 5–9 years)

  4 Practising speed and fluency (lower Key Stage 2 / 7–9 years)

  5 Presentation skills (upper Key Stage 2 / 10–11 years)

3 Handwriting must be actively taught: this can be done in association with spelling. Learning to associate the kinaesthetic handwriting movement with the visual letter pattern and the aural phonemes will help children with learning to spell.

A practical approach

Penpals offers a practical approach to support the delivery of handwriting teaching in the context of the modern curriculum:

- **Time** *Penpals'* focus on whole-class teaching, with key teaching points clearly identified, allows effective teaching in the time available.
- **Planning** *Penpals* helps with long-, medium- and short-term planning for each key stage, correlated to national guidelines.
- **Practice** *Penpals* offers pupil Practice Books with their own internal structure of excellent models for independent writing.
- **Revision** *Penpals* offers opportunities for record-keeping, review and assessment throughout the course.
- **Motivation** The *Penpals* materials are attractive and well-designed. They were written with the support of handwriting experts to stimulate and motivate children.
- **ICT** Use the *Penpals* CD-ROMs to enrich and extend children's handwriting experiences.

A few words from the experts...

Professor Rhona Stainthorp *Professor, Institute of Education, University of Reading*

We now know that if children are to achieve comfortable, legible, flexible handwriting styles, they need to be taught to form and join each letter efficiently. *Penpals* sets out to achieve this. Children need good models to copy, lots of practice and feedback to help them fine-tune their performance.

If the practice element of letter formation includes the practice of spelling patterns, as in *Penpals*, the resultant pedagogy addresses two of the essential sub-skills of good written communication, namely handwriting and spelling.

Efficient handwriting leads to higher-quality writing.

Dr Rosemary Sassoon *Handwriting expert*

The Sassoon family of typefaces has been used throughout this scheme. Many people might therefore describe them as the model but they are typefaces, not exactly a handwriting model. No hand could copy them exactly and be so consistent and invariable. Equally, no typeface, however many alternative letters and joins are built in to a font, can be quite as flexible as handwritten letters. Our letters represent the movement, proportions and clear characteristics of basic separate and joined letters. It is likely that every teacher will produce his or her own slightly different version on the whiteboard, and pupils will then do likewise. It matters little if the slant or proportions of a child's writing differ slightly from any model. We are not teaching children to be forgers. We are equipping them with an efficient, legible handwriting that will serve them all their life – one that suits their hand and their personality. Flexibility is stressed throughout this scheme.

Sue Palmer *Literacy specialist and educational writer*

Penpals materials provide everything necessary for structured teaching of handwriting in the junior years. Frequent links to other literacy objectives for the age group mean handwriting lessons also become an opportunity to revise other aspects of writing at word, sentence and text level.

Links to national guidelines

Penpals Year 4/Primary 5 supports many national guidelines including:

- *The National Curriculum for England and Wales*;
- *Primary Framework for literacy and mathematics* (Primary National Strategy 2006);
- *English Language 5–14 Guidelines* (The Scottish Office – Education Department);
- *The Northern Ireland Curriculum: Primary* (CCEA).

Using handwriting across the curriculum

By Y4/P5, most children are beginning to write fluently, and they should be encouraged to incorporate joining into their cross-curricular writing. Medium-frequency words are included in the Practice Book pages wherever possible. (In Y4/P5, the high-frequency words covered are: *above, almost, always, animals, asked, balloon, before, began, better, birthday, brought, can't, clothes, didn't, different, does, don't, eyes, first, follow, friends, garden, goes, gone, great, happy, head, I'm, important, jumped, know, light, money, morning, near, never, number, opened, right, round, second, small, sometimes, sound, starting, stopped, sure, swimming, think, through, today, together, tries, under, upon, walking, why, window, woke, world, year, young.*) If appropriate, set handwriting targets for the children and incorporate cross-curricular writing into handwriting assessments.

Classroom organisation

The ideal classroom organisation for teaching *Penpals* is to have the children sitting at desks or tables arranged so that they can all see the interactive white board (IWB). Each child needs a dry-wipe board (preferably with guidelines) and a marker pen, or pencil and paper.

If this organisation is not possible within your classroom, bear in mind the following points as you plan your own classroom:

- All the children need to see the IWB and be able to copy words or handwriting patterns from it.
- Handwriting is usually done on a horizontal or slightly sloped surface.

When to use *Penpals*

Penpals can be used flexibly to teach handwriting. Ideally the whole-class teaching session will be followed immediately by the independent work but, where this is not possible, the sessions may be split.

Timing the sessions

The whole-class session for each unit, including the warm-up activities, should take no more than 15 minutes. The independent working session should take about 15–20 minutes.

In addition to the allocated time, extra daily 'practice times' of 5–10 minutes are ideal, if the practicalities of your timetable allow for it. Children can use these sessions to practise the high-frequency words, to extend their pattern practice or to revisit the letter pattern shown in the Practice Book. As with most successful learning, 'little and often' is the most effective approach.

Penpals for Handwriting: Y4 © Gill Budgell (Frattempo) and Kate Ruttle 2009

Sequence for teaching the units

Gross and fine motor skills

The shape of the lower Key Stage 2 (Primary 4 and 5) lessons generally follow a common pattern:

In Y3 and 4 (P4 and 5) of *Penpals*, 10 units have been provided for each school term. The units have been organised into a specific teaching sequence to ensure that skills are developed, practised and consolidated and that relevant spelling patterns can be used. However, if it fits better with your spelling programme, you may wish to alter the order in which the children complete the units, particularly in Terms 1 and 3.

Teaching sequence for a unit of *Penpals for Handwriting*

You will need:

- the Year 4 CD-ROM;
- the relevant Teacher's Book page;
- the Big Book or water-based marker pens for annotating the pages.

Children will need:

- dry-wipe boards and marker pens* or pencils and paper;
- pencils, or pens if you wish to practise writing in ink;
- the relevant Practice Book;
- handwriting exercise book.

(*Remember that one of the crucial elements of ensuring good handwriting is good posture. If children are writing with dry-wipe boards on their knees or on the floor, good posture is more difficult to achieve.)

Whole-class session

1 **Warm up** These ideas complement the gross and fine motor control warm-up clips accessible from the main menu of the CD-ROM. Use these at the start of the lesson to prepare the upper part of the body and the hands for handwriting.

2 **Unit focus and spelling/ vocabulary link** These are clearly identified at the start of each unit.

4 **Letter/join animations** These provide opportunities to demonstrate and talk about correct letter/join formation. Children can practise tracing and copying the letters/joins.

5 **Artwork** These pictures represent a word relating to the focus join. Children identify the word and the relationship.

3 **Units** Every unit begins with a whole-class teaching session based on the CD-ROM.

7 **Group work** Guidance for using the Big Book page with small groups to reinforce modelling the focus letters/joins in the context of longer texts.

8 **Independent work** See page 7.

6 **Word bank** These activities provide banks of differentiated words that you can use to model and discuss letter/join formation. Children can practise tracing the target letter/joins in words.

Independent work

This session can follow on directly from the whole-class session. Ideally, children's work should be overseen by an adult to ensure correct formation and joining, especially for those about whom you have concerns. The teacher's page for the unit provides helpful advice on using the Practice Book page together.

At Key Stage 1 and Key Stage 2, children will need a handwriting exercise book to record their work in. They should have a sharpened pencil for their writing, but may also need coloured pencils for pattern practice.

The Practice Book pages offer:

Independent writing Practice of the focus join or joins.

Copying joins in context Once the children have practised writing the joins, they should try to write them in a context (usually a simple phrase or sentence, joke or rhyme).

Pattern practice Children will need to practise the patterns at the bottom of the page. These usually reflect the pencil movement of the unit focus, but always enhance fine motor control. These patterns can be made using coloured pencils. The patterns are artwork, not letters, and should be treated as opportunities to develop movement and control.

Also in the Teacher's Book:

Take aways These are photocopy masters (PCMs) for extra practice or homework.

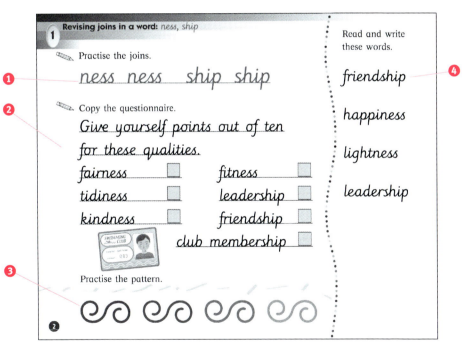

High-frequency words Look, Say, Cover, Write, Check practice is provided for high-frequency words that feature the unit focus join (where possible).

Differentiation using *Penpals* can be achieved in a number of ways:

- Children working individually with a Teaching Assistant may benefit from additional practice on dry-wipe boards.
- Take away activities provide excellent opportunities for differentiation as detailed above. Cross-references to similar Take aways in earlier books can help you to select less challenging activities for those who need extra practice at a lower level.
- Higher-achieving children can be challenged by higher expectations of control and evenness of letters.

Assessment and record-keeping

On-going formative assessment

The most effective assessment of handwriting is on-going assessment because this gives you the chance to spot any errors or inconsistencies that are likely to impede a fast, fluent hand in the future. Be especially aware of left-handers and the difference between a pencil hold that will seriously limit their success in the future and one that has been found to work efficiently.

At Key Stage 2, a starting-point assessment PCM is provided for use at the beginning of each school year (see page 9). This assesses the previous year's work and gives an indication of what needs to be consolidated before beginning new work.

The Practice Book page annotations in the Teacher's Book enable you to draw the children's attention to key handwriting issues.

Summative assessment

Beginning of year

The PCM on page 9 can be used for an assessment to ensure that all children are ready for *Penpals: Y4/P5*. If children's joining is still insecure, they will benefit from revisiting units in *Penpals: Y3/P4*.

End of year

You can use text from Unit 29 as the basis of a summative assessment. As you do the summative assessment, consider key handwriting issues:

- Are all letters formed correctly?
- Are letters consistently sized?
- Are known joins used?
- Are they used correctly?
- Are ascenders and descenders parallel?
- Are spaces within and between words regular?
- Are joined and print scripts used correctly?
- Is good handwriting carried over into cross-curricular activities?
- What are the next handwriting targets for this child?

Record-keeping

- The best record of what children have achieved will be in their handwriting books. It is therefore important to keep a book specifically for this purpose. This will provide a useful record of achievement to share with parents and colleagues.
- The Contents page can be photocopied and used with highlighting pens and dates to keep a record of which units have been completed. You may find it helpful to use a 'traffic light' system (green highlighter pen for 'achieved', yellow for 'not totally secure' and pink for 'not achieved') to highlight units you need to revisit with individuals, groups or the whole class.

Children's beginning of year assessment

Name .... Date ....

Copy these joins and these words. Then copy the book titles.

ld	_____	would	_____
py	_____	happy	_____
bo	_____	bottle	_____
pa	_____	party	_____
bi	_____	biscuit	_____
pu	_____	puddle	_____
ph	_____	graph	_____
bl	_____	black	_____

Parachute Jumping by Hugo First

Holidays Abroad by Sandie Beaches

Modern Giants by Hugh Mungous

Glossary of key terms

Talking about handwriting

Throughout *Penpals* it has been assumed that correct terminology should be used as soon as possible.

Terms used in *Penpals* include:

- **Gross motor skills, fine motor skills.**
- **Lower case letter.**
- **Capital letter** is used in preference to 'upper case letter'.
- **Short letter** is the term used to describe a letter with no ascender or descender.
- **Letter with an ascender, letter with a descender.**
- **Flick** is used to describe an exit stroke (note that *t* finishes with a curl to the right rather than merely an exit flick).
- **Curve** is used to describe a descender on letters (*y, j, g, f*).
- **Cross bar** is used to describe the left-to-right line on *t* and *f*. It may also be used in relation to letters that feature a left-to-right horizontal line (e.g. *e* and *z*).
- **Diagonal join to ascender** (e.g. *at*), **diagonal join (no ascender)** (e.g. *du*), **diagonal join to an anticlockwise letter** (e.g. *ho*).
- **Horizontal join to ascender** (e.g. *oh*), **horizontal join (no ascender)** (e.g. *re*), **horizontal join to an anticlockwise letter** (e.g. *wo*).
- Other important terminology used throughout *Penpals* includes **vertical**, **parallel**, **joined**, **sloped**.

Key CD-ROM features

- **Warm-up clips** These activities may be linked to the focus of the unit but are generally just enjoyable movement activities to warm up the muscles.
- **Letter/join animations** These animations encourage the children to watch and sky write as the focus letter/join animates on the screen.
- **Word bank** This provides a useful bank of words that enable you to demonstrate the focus letters/joins.
- **Show alphabet** These animations show how to form all capital and lower case letters.
- **Library of joins** These animations show correct formation of key joins.

Notes on formation of specific letters and joins

Correct letter formation can be demonstrated using the **Show alphabet** section on the CD-ROM.

- *k* – the use of the curly form of *k*, as opposed to the straight *k*, is recommended by handwriting experts because its flowing form lends itself more naturally to joining. It is also more easily distinguished from the capital letter.
- *o* – there is no exit stroke from the lower case *o* when it is not joined. Unlike the flick at the bottom of letters like *n* and *l*, the exit stroke from the *o* is not an integral part of the letter, but simply a mechanism for joining.
- *e* – two different forms of *e* (*e*/*e*) are used in order to show children how it alters when other letters are joined to it.
- *f, q, r, s* – letters that the children are taught to join in Y2/P3.
- *b* and *p* – letters that the children are taught to join in Y3/P4.
  Handwriting is generally faster and more legible if it is not continuously joined.
- *g, j, y* – letters that are not joined from, though there is some exploration of joining them in Y5 & 6 / P6 & 7.
- *x* and *z* – we do not join to or from *x* or *z* as these are uncomfortable joins that often result in the malformation of both the joining letter and the *x* or *z*.

Capitals

It is generally agreed that there is no right or wrong way to form capitals. However, there is a general principle of forming them from top to bottom and left to right wherever possible. As skills and confidence develop, left-handers may well form capitals differently (they have a tendency to go from right to left, for example). This should not be an issue as capitals are never joined.

- **Capital Y**: the use of a central stalk (as opposed to a slanting stalk) is recommended as once children have completed the 'v' form at the top of the letter, they have a clear starting point for the downwards stroke. This formation also distinguishes the capital letter from the lower case letter and retains its shape when written at speed.
- **Capital G**: this form of *G* is recommended as the correct handwriting form of the letter. Variations which include a vertical line (*G*) are font forms.
- **Capital H**: the formation of *H* using two down strokes followed by the horizontal stroke from left to right is recommended. The alternative (one down stroke followed by a horizontal and a further down stroke) can quickly resemble the letter *M* when written at speed.
- **Capital K**: the formation of *K* with two pencil strokes rather than three is recommended as it is more fluently formed when writing at speed.

In order to promote fluent handwriting and to support the early stages of spelling, some handwriting joins are introduced in Y1/P2 as soon as all individual letter formation is secure.

By the time they are using the Y4/P5 resources, children should be becoming secure and confident with the common joins and beginning to use them for all 'neat' writing activities. The emphasis in these resources is on developing an even, fluent handwriting style, ensuring consistency in size and proportion of letters, and the spacing between letters and words.

Progression in the introduction of joins

Y1/P2 In these resources only two or three letters in a word are joined. The words on the CD-ROM and in the Big Book and the Practice Book feature the focus join for the teaching unit.

Y2/P3 As more joins are introduced, children are given opportunities to practise familiar joins which are not the focus of the unit. During the year, children are expected to begin to join all the letters in a short word, or to join letter patterns which can support spelling.

Y3&4/P4&5 All the basic joins will now be familiar. In these resources, children are asked to practise 'tricky joins' and to begin to develop fluent, even handwriting. An emphasis on spacing between letters and words, consistency of letter size, and parallel ascenders and descenders helps children to present their work well.

Y4/P5 Children are introduced to a sloped style of writing and are expected to write mostly in pen. Children are also introduced to the print alphabet for purposes such as captions, labels, headings and posters.

The sequence for *Penpals: Y4/P5* is:

Term 1   Revising joins in a word.
             Linking spelling and handwriting.
Term 2   Introducing sloped writing.
             Parallel ascenders and descenders in sloped writing.
             Space, size and proportion in sloped writing.
             Speed and fluency in sloped writing.
Term 3   Further practice of key issues in sloped writing.
             Print alphabet and capitals.
             Assessment.

Y5&6/P6&7 Two sets of OHTs are provided for each of these year groups, one with a handwriting focus, the other with a project focus.

Defining the joins

(See the inside back cover of this Teacher's Book for a full list of letter sets requiring each of the joins as taught in Y4/P5.)

The two basic join types

- **Diagonal join** (e.g. *at*) (introduced in Y1/P2, Unit 11): this is the most common join. It starts from the final flick on the baseline (or 'curl' in the case of the letter *t*). Letters that come before a diagonal join are: *a*, *b*, *c*, *d*, *e*, *h*, *i*, *k*, *l*, *m*, *n*, *p*, *s*, *t*, *u* (and *q*, in which the flick begins below the baseline).
- **Horizontal join** (e.g. *op*) (introduced in Y1/P2, Unit 24): this join is formed from letters that finish at the top of the letter rather than at the baseline. Letters that come before a horizontal join are: *f*, *o*, *r*, *v*, *w*.

Variations on the join types

Penpals uses three subsets of the main joins: join to a letter with an ascender, join to a letter with no ascender and join to a letter that begins with an anticlockwise movement. Since the last subset involves stopping the pencil and reversing the direction of movement, these are called *diagonal join to an anticlockwise letter* and *horizontal join to an anticlockwise letter*. Joins to anticlockwise letters are trickier to teach and need more practice than straightforward horizontal and diagonal joins. These joins tend to 'decay' when children begin to write more quickly.

- **Diagonal join to a letter with an ascender** (e.g. *ub*) (introduced in Y1/P2, Unit 11): this is a variation of the diagonal join.
- **Diagonal join to an anticlockwise letter** (e.g. *ho*) (introduced in Y1/P2, Unit 18): joining with a diagonal join to the anticlockwise letters in the 'curly caterpillar' family involves stopping the hand movement and reversing it. This can be a tricky join and it decays easily in fast writing.
- **Horizontal join to an anticlockwise letter** (e.g. *wo*) (introduced in Y1/P2, Unit 26): joining from a horizontal join to an anticlockwise letter involves a reversal.
- **Horizontal join to a letter with an ascender** (e.g. *oh*) (introduced in Y1/P2, Unit 28): this is a slightly sloped version of a horizontal join.
- **Break letters** (introduced in Y2/P3): these are letters from which no join has yet been taught. (See notes on page 10.)

Correct formation of key joins can be demonstrated using the **Library of joins** section on the CD-ROM.

Join patter for *Penpals*

This chart shows the oral patter for the formation of joins.

Diagonal join to ascender: *at, all*	Slope all the way up from the flick to begin the next letter.
Diagonal join, no ascender	Slope up from the flick to begin the next letter.
Diagonal join, no ascender, to an anticlockwise letter	Slope up from the flick and round to begin the curve.
Horizontal join, no ascender	Across from the top to begin the next letter.
Horizontal join, no ascender, to an anticlockwise letter	Across from the top and round to begin the curve.
Horizontal join to ascender	Across from the top and slope all the way up to begin the next letter.
Diagonal join to ascender, to an anticlockwise letter	Slope all the way up from the flick and round to begin the curve.
Horizontal join to ascender, to an anticlockwise letter	Across from the top and all the way up and round to begin the curve.
Break letters	Lift and start the next letter.
Horizontal join from *r* to ascender	Over and dip, and slope all the way up to begin the next letter.
Horizontal join from *r*	Over and dip to begin the next letter.
Diagonal join to *s*	Slope up from the flick and round to begin a 'small curve' *s*.
Horizontal join to *s*	Across from the top, dip and round to begin a 'small curve' *s*.
Diagonal join from *s* to ascender	Swing all the way up from the bottom curve to begin the next letter.
Diagonal join from *s*, no ascender	Swing up from the bottom curve to begin the next letter.
Horizontal join from *r* to an anticlockwise letter	Over and dip, and round to begin the curve.
Horizontal join (to and) from *f* to ascender	Across the bar and slope all the way up to begin the next letter.
Horizontal join from *f*, no ascender	Across the bar to begin the next letter.
qu	Slope up from the flick to begin the *u*.
rr	Over and dip to begin the next letter.
ss	Swing up from the bottom curve to begin a 'small curve' *s*.
ff	Across the bar and slope all the way up and round to begin the curve.
Joining *b* and *p*	Swing up from the bottom curve to begin the next letter.

When you introduce *Penpals* into your school, it is important to ensure that all the staff in the school follow the scheme. Suggestions are given on page 11 to support the introduction of the programme throughout the school as there may be some issues for children who have not met joining before. To do this, it may be useful to hold an INSET staff meeting. The following pages in this book are photocopiable to make OHTs for this purpose:

- page 14 – outline of INSET session;
- page 15 – information sheet for parents;
- page 16 – variations of the font;
- pages 62 and 63 – handwriting mats;
- page 64 – photocopiable ruled sheet for handwriting practice;
- inside back cover – joining letter sets (also appears on the inside front cover of the Big Book and Practice Book).

Suggested topics for inclusion in INSET meeting

Organisational issues

- **Rationale for introducing *Penpals for Handwriting*** Use the information on page 4.
- **Classroom organisation** Copy page 5 of this introduction for all staff. Read through it together, agreeing on the most appropriate time for the sessions, etc.
- **Assessment and record-keeping** Use the information on page 8.
- **Home–school links** Make an OHT of the information sheet on page 14.

Handwriting issues

- **Font** Use the **Show alphabet** section on the CD-ROM to demonstrate the font. Information on page 10 of the introduction may be used to clarify any issues arising.
- **Font size** Photocopy page 16 of this Teacher's Book to demonstrate how font size is shown throughout *Penpals*.
- **Joins and break letters** Use the **Show joining letter sets** section on the CD-ROM, or an OHT of the inside back cover of this book, to demonstrate the joining letter sets and the break letters.
- **Writing on lined paper** Children should be encouraged to write on lined paper from the time they begin to focus on correct letter formation and orientation. As the children's handwriting becomes more controlled, the width between the lines should decrease. It may well be that at any given time different children in your class will benefit from writing on paper with different line widths. The size of the font in the Practice Books is intended to reflect a development in handwriting. However, you should still tailor the handwriting materials to meet the needs of individual children in your class. A photocopiable sheet with lines of a suitable width is provided on page 64. Some children may prefer to write on lined paper which also includes guidelines for the height of ascenders and descenders.
- **Pencil hold** Use the pencil hold videos in the **Posture clips** section on the CD-ROM to illustrate good pencil hold. The traditionally recommended pencil hold allows children to sustain handwriting for long periods without tiring their hands. However, there are many alternative pencil holds (particularly for left-handers) and the most important thing is comfort and a hold that will be efficient under speed. Some children may benefit from triangular pencils or ordinary pencils with plastic pencil grips.

- **Posture** Use the photographs in the **Posture clips** section on the CD-ROM to illustrate good posture. A good posture and pencil hold are vital for good handwriting. Although many young children enjoy sitting on one foot, kneeling or wrapping their feet around the legs of the chair, they will find it easier to sustain good handwriting comfortably if they adopt a good posture.
- **Left-handed children** Left-handed children should not sit to the right of right-handed children as their papers will meet in the middle! Left-handed children should be taught to position their paper to the left of centre and then angle the paper for comfort as suggested below. Use the left-handed pencil hold video and posture photograph in the **Posture clips** section on the CD-ROM to illustrate this. There is no reason why left-handed children's handwriting should be any worse than that of right-handed children.
- **Sloped surfaces** Children who experience some motor control difficulties often benefit from writing on a slight slope. The easiest and cheapest way to provide this in the classroom is to use substantial A4 or foolscap ring-binders of which there are usually plenty in school. Commercial wooden or plastic writing slopes are also widely available.
- **Angle of paper** Make an OHT of the guidelines to illustrate good positions for right- or left-handed children as provided on pages 62 and 63. If children still need help with choosing a good angle for their paper while they are writing, you can photocopy these onto A3 paper and laminate them to make table-top mats. Use the spaces provided to allow children to find the optimum position. Show the children how to line up the corners of their books to create a comfortable angle for writing, or how to use Blu-Tack to secure paper to the mats to produce guidelines when writing on blank paper. These guidelines provide a good guide, but encourage the children to explore personal variation of the angles.

Organisational issues

- ## Rationale
  - a flexible, fluent and legible handwriting style
  - a 5-stage developmental process
  - active teaching in association with phonics and spelling

- ## Classroom organisation
  - weekly teaching sessions with little-and-often practice

- ## Assessment and record-keeping
  - beginning of year assessment for each year group
  - encourages self-assessment

- ## Home–school links
  - parent information sheets for each year
  - homework activities

Handwriting issues

font, font size, joins and break letters, writing on lined paper, pencil hold, posture, left-handed children, sloped surfaces, angle of paper

Penpals for Handwriting: Year 4 information sheet for parents

The main aims during this year are for children to begin to slope their handwriting and to make sure that the size and proportions of all letters, and the spaces between letters and words, are consistent and even. Attention is also given to keeping ascenders and descenders parallel.

Formation of capitals and lower case letters should now be familiar and secure.

Children have been introduced to the two basic join types:

- Joins from the baseline, known as **diagonal joins**, including:
  - diagonal join to a short letter, e.g. *mm, nn*
  - diagonal join to an ascender, e.g. *tt, ll*
  - diagonal join to an anticlockwise letter, e.g. *ic, ss*
- Joins from the cross bar, known as **horizontal joins**, including:
  - horizontal join to a short letter, e.g. *ou, on*
  - horizontal join to an ascender, e.g. *ot, wh, fl*
  - horizontal join to an anticlockwise letter, e.g. *oo, wa, fa*

Break letters (i.e. letters which are not joined from at this stage) include *g, j* and *y*. Letters which are never joined to or from are *x* and *z*.

By this stage, children should be secure at joining and able to use joined-up writing for most of their work. Children will be beginning to practise writing in ink.

Opportunities will also be provided for children to practise writing at increased speed so that they can produce longer pieces of writing with greater ease.

There is continued emphasis on using the movements of handwriting to support spelling through the revision of common letter patterns.

Children will be introduced to the print alphabet for purposes such as captions, headings, labels and posters.

Variations in font throughout *Penpals*

FIVE DEVELOPMENTAL PHASES	SASSOON® CAMBRIDGE JOINER	*Penpals* Progression	*Penpals* typesizes*
1 GROSS AND FINE MOTOR SKILLS AND LETTER FORMATION	*a*	Each letter family is introduced with finger tracing letters incorporating the letter family artwork and a starting dot.	*a a* **Foundation 2/Primary 1** 21mm/11.5mm
	b	Hollow letters with starting dots and arrows to show correct letter formation are also used for finger tracing.	*a a* **Year 1/Primary 2** 17mm/8mm
	c	Solid letters with starting dots support letter formation.	*a* **Year 2/Primary 3** 5.5mm
	d	Independent writing with exit flicks is encouraged in preparation for joining.	*a* **Year 3/Primary 4** 4mm
2 BEGINNING TO JOIN	*pen*	Red is used for the focus join and joining letters to teach fluent formation.	*a* **Year 4 onwards/Primary 5 onwards** sloped, 4mm
3 SECURING THE JOINS	*secure*	Once all joins have been taught, all words are shown as joined for practice and consolidation.	
4 PRACTISING SPEED AND FLUENCY	*faster*	Children are encouraged to develop an individual style for speed and legibility.	
5 PRESENTATION SKILLS	*individual* **print** *jokey*	Further development of an individual style as well as presentation skills and techniques.	

* Letters in red are for finger tracing. Letters in black are writing models.

Penpals for Handwriting: Y4

1 Revising joins in a word: *ness, ship*

Warm up

 Ask the children to put their hands on their laps. When you say 'quick' they should lift their hands as high as they can and as quickly as they can. When you say 'slow' they should move their hands as slowly as possible, but with great control. Let them practise raising and lowering their hands and arms as you say 'quick' and 'slow'.

 Children repeat the above exercise with their fingers.

CD-ROM

Unit focus: revising joins in a word.
Spelling link: suffixes **ness** and **ship**.

Artwork
Children try to identify a word with one of the target letter patterns represented by the artwork.

Join animations
Reinforce the flowing movement in these familiar joins. Check that letter size and appropriate spacing are maintained.

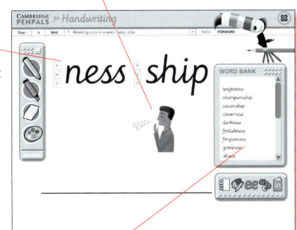

Word bank
Choose one of the words to revise joins using the suffixes *ness* and *ship*. Click on the word to make the join grey for modelling and discussion.

Group work

Introduce the page
● Read the speech bubbles. Explain that you're going to recap the work on joining letters in words that you did last year. Remind the children of the spelling link (*ness*, *ship*), and of spelling work done in the past.

Demonstrate the unit focus
● Demonstrate tracing over the words in grey, emphasising the smooth movement of your hand as you do so.
● Remind children of some of the key issues, such as the fact that capitals don't join, *g* and *y* are break letters, ascenders and descenders should be parallel, and that the spacing and size of letters should be consistent.

   Show Me Children practise writing the words.

● Can the children suggest other words that include these suffixes? (e.g. *friendliness, kindness, hardship, leadership*) Model writing these up.

   Show Me Children practise writing these words too.

Big Book page 2

Independent work

Watch while children copy the joins. ❶

Ensure that children understand that this is a ❷ magazine-style personality questionnaire. Encourage the children to read the instruction and the questionnaire before they copy it. Make sure they attempt to join the appropriate parts of the word with a fluid movement. After children have finished copying, let them fill in the boxes with their scores.

Encourage children to practise the pattern in the bottom panel.

Can the children look, say, cover, write and check these words?

Practice Book page 2

Take away

① For additional practice of joining use **PCM 1**.

② If children find any joins particularly hard, refer back to the **PCM** covering that join type in **Years 1–3**.

Warm up

🖐 Children tuck their chins in and roll their heads round clockwise and anticlockwise.

🖐 Children rotate their wrists clockwise and anticlockwise.

CD-ROM

Unit focus: revising joins in a word.

Spelling link: regular verb endings **ing** and **ed**.

Artwork

Children try to identify a word with one of the target letter patterns represented by the artwork.

Join animations

Reinforce the flowing movement in these familiar joins. Check that letter size and appropriate spacing are maintained.

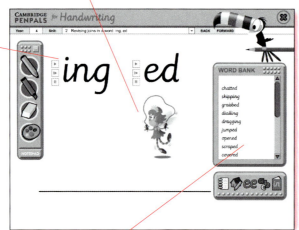

Word bank

Choose one of the words to revise joins in *ing* and *ed*. Click on the word to make the join grey for modelling and discussion.

Group work

Introduce the page

● Read the text, making sure children understand it's about two people in very different places. Explain that you're going to do some more practice of joining using verbs ending in *ing* and *ed*. Remind the children of spelling work done in the past.

Demonstrate the unit focus

● Demonstrate tracing over the words in grey, emphasising the smooth movement of your hand as you do so.

  Show Me Children practise writing the words in grey. Ensure that the ascenders are parallel in the words *blowing* and *hailed*.

● Can the children suggest other verbs that end in *ing* and *ed*? (e.g. *running, jumping, stayed, walked*) Model writing these up.

  Show Me Children practise writing these words too.

Big Book page 3

Independent work

Watch while children copy the joins. ➊

Encourage the children to read the rubric and the poem. Make sure they attempt to join the appropriate parts of the words with a fluid movement. ➋

Practice Book page 3

Encourage children to practise the pattern in the bottom panel. ➍ ➌

Can the children look, say, cover, write and check these words?

Take away

① For additional practice of joining use **PCM 2**.

② If children find any joins particularly hard, refer back to the **PCM** covering that join type in **Years 1–3**.

3 Revising joins in a word: *s*

Warm up

👋 Children cross their arms, raise them up high, then shake them out.

👋 Ask the children to make rings by touching their forefingers to their thumbs. Can they make these rings interlock? (e.g. by touching the thumb and finger of their right hand inside the ring made by the thumb and finger of their left hand) Let them make interlocking rings using each finger in turn touching their thumbs.

CD-ROM

Unit focus: revising joins in a word.

Spelling link: regular verb ending **s**.

Artwork

Children try to identify a word with the target letter pattern represented by the artwork.

Letter animation

Reinforce the flowing movement in this letter.

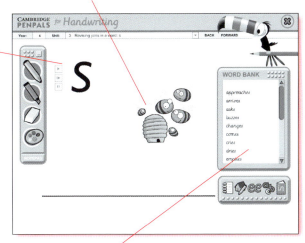

Word bank

Choose one of the words to revise joins to and from *s*. Click on the word to make the joins grey for modelling and discussion.

Group work

Introduce the page

● Read the piece, making sure children understand it's a sports commentary in the present tense. Explain that you're going to do some more practice of joining with a focus on *s*. Remind the children of spelling work done in the past.

Demonstrate the unit focus

Get Up and Go Ask children to circle the present tense verbs ending in *s* (*passes, tackles, keeps, dribbles, heads, speeds, shoots, scores*).

● Demonstrate writing these words, emphasising the smooth movement of your hand as you do so.

● Now model writing the word *possession*, pointing out the two sets of double *s*.

Show Me Children practise writing the words. Ensure that the ascenders are parallel in the words *tackles, dribbles, heads* and *shoots*, and that the spacing around the *s* is appropriate.

● Can the children suggest other verbs ending in *s*? (e.g. *moves, jumps, runs, shouts*) Model writing these up.

Show Me Children practise writing these words too.

Independent work

Watch while children copy the joins. **1**

Encourage the children to read the rubric. If **2** necessary, remind them of the spelling rules they will need to follow when completing the word sums. (Change *y* to *i* and add *es*, and add *es* when the root verb ends with a hissing sound.) Make sure they attempt to join the appropriate parts of the words with a fluid movement.

Encourage children to practise the pattern in the bottom panel.

Can the children look, say, cover, write and check these medium-frequency words?

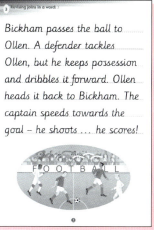

Practice Book page 4

Take away

① For additional practice of joining use **PCM 3**.

② If children find any joins particularly hard, refer back to the **PCM** covering that join type in **Years 1–3**.

Bickham passes the ball to Ollen. A defender tackles Ollen, but he keeps possession and dribbles it forward. Ollen heads it back to Bickham. The captain speeds towards the goal – he shoots … he scores!

FOOTBALL

Big Book page 4

4 Revising joins in a word: *ify*

Warm up

- 👆 Let children stand up, stretch their arms out in front of them and shut their eyes. Can they bring each finger in turn to touch their nose, ears or forehead?
- ✋ Children close their eyes and touch each finger of the opposite hand with their forefinger as fast as they can.

CD-ROM

Unit focus: revising joins in a word.
Vocabulary link: to make nouns and adjectives into verbs by adding **ify**.

Artwork
Children try to identify a word with the target letter pattern represented by the artwork.

Join animation
Reinforce the flowing movement in these familiar joins. Check that joins to and from *f* are correctly formed.

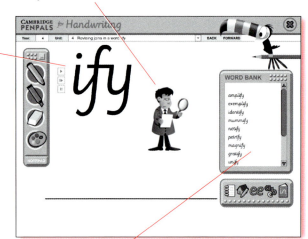

Word bank
Choose one of the words to revise joins in *ify*. Click on the word to make the joins grey for modelling and discussion.

Group work

Introduce the page
- Look at the page, reading out the first sentence as follows: 'If I can make it pure I can purify it'. Explain that you're going to practise writing some verbs made from adjectives and the ending *ify*. Remind children of spelling work done in the past.

Demonstrate the unit focus
- Read out the next sentence, pausing so that children can supply the answer: 'If I can make it beautiful I can …' (*beautify it*).
- Ask for suggestions of how to spell the word if appropriate to your class and model writing it up. Continue with the remaining words.

  Show Me Children practise writing the words. Check that the joins to and from *f* are correctly formed.

- Can the children suggest other verbs ending in *ify*? (e.g. *classify, verify, quantify, notify*) Model writing these up.

  Show Me Children practise writing these words too.

If I can …   I can …

make it pure
                    purify it
make it beautiful

make it clear

make it solid

make it glorious

Big Book page 5

Independent work

Watch while children copy the joins. **①**

Encourage the children to read the rubric and the instructions. Make sure they attempt to join the appropriate parts of the words with a fluid movement. **②**

Encourage children to practise the pattern in the bottom panel.

Can the children look, say, cover, write and check these words?

Practice Book page 5

Take away

① For additional practice of joining use **PCM 4**.

② If children find any joins particularly hard, refer back to the **PCM** covering that join type in **Years 1–3**.

5 Revising joins in a word: *nn*, *mm*, *ss*

Big Book page 6

Warm up

- Children alternately fold their arms then stretch them out to the sides and above their heads.
- Ask children to make fists with both their hands, then stretch their hands as wide as they will go before making fists again. They can repeat this movement several times.

CD-ROM

Unit focus: revising joins in a word.
Spelling link: two-syllable words containing double consonants.

Artwork
Children try to identify a word with one of the target letter patterns represented by the artwork.

Join animations
Reinforce the flowing movement in these familiar joins. Check that joins to and from *s* are correctly formed.

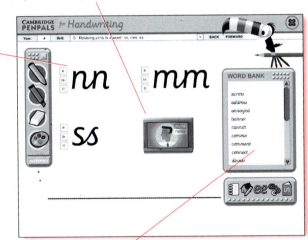

Word bank
Choose one of the words to revise the *nn*, *mm* and *ss* joins. Click on the word to make the join grey for modelling and discussion.

Group work

Introduce the page
- Look at the page, and read through the poster. Explain you're going to do some more practice of joining two-syllable words with an emphasis on double consonants *nn*, *mm*, *ss*. Remind children of spelling work done in the past.

Demonstrate the unit focus
- Model tracing over the words in grey. Emphasise the fluidity of the movement and the even sizing of all the letters.
  Show Me Children practise writing the words. On the *ss*, check that the first letter is completed correctly before the pencil stroke is reversed to write the second letter.
- Can the children suggest other words featuring the letter patterns *nn*, *mm*, *ss*? (e.g. *winner*, *swimmer*, *fussy*) Model writing these up.
  Show Me Children practise writing these words too.

Independent work

Watch while children copy the joins. **1**

Encourage the children to read the rubric. **2**
Make sure they don't spend too much time copying the table. If necessary, remind them of the need to double the consonant in *skim, scan, fan, hum* and *slam* when adding the endings.

Practice Book page 6

Encourage children to practise the pattern in the bottom panel. **3**

Can the children look, say, cover, write and check these words? **4**

Take away

① For additional practice of joining use **PCM 5**.
② If children find any joins particularly hard, refer back to the **PCM** covering that join type in **Years 1–3**.

6 Revising parallel ascenders: *tt*, *ll*, *bb*

Warm up

👆 Children point their arms up vertically above their heads, then bend their arms at the elbows, so that their hands go behind their heads.

👆 Children should point both their forefingers straight up vertically, bend them in the middle, then straighten them horizontally. They can repeat this movement up to five times with different fingers.

CD-ROM

Unit focus: revising parallel ascenders.
Spelling link: two-syllable words containing double consonants.

Artwork
Children try to identify a word with one of the target letter patterns represented by the artwork.

Join animations
Reinforce the flowing movement in these familiar joins. Check that all ascenders are parallel and the same height.

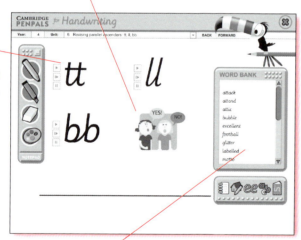

Word bank
Choose one of the words to revise parallel ascenders using the *tt*, *ll* and *bb* joins. Click on the word to make the join grey for modelling and discussion.

Group work

Introduce the page
- Look at the page and read through the menu. Yuk! Explain you're going to do some practice of joining two-syllable words with an emphasis on double consonants with ascenders *tt*, *ll*, *bb*. Remind children of spelling work done in the past.

Demonstrate the unit focus
- Model tracing over the words in grey, emphasising the fluidity of the movement, the even size of the letters and the parallel ascenders.
- Point out that when writing the word *rattlesnake*, you still cross the double *t* when you've written the whole word.

  Show Me Children practise writing some of the words. Check that their ascenders are parallel.

- Can the children suggest other horrible foods featuring the letter patterns *tt*, *ll* or *bb*? (e.g. *bottled sour buttermilk*)

  Show Me Children practise writing these words too.

Big Book page 7

Independent work

Watch while children copy the joins. **1**

Encourage the children to read the rubric. **2** Check that the ascenders are parallel in the words they write. (Some rhyming words to suggest in case anyone gets stuck: *pillow, wobble, mitten, holly, bubble, chatter, rattle, hollow, lobbed*).

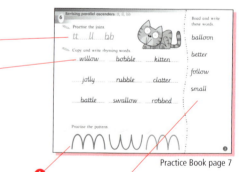
Practice Book page 7

Encourage children to practise the pattern in the bottom panel. **3**

Can the children look, say, cover, write and check these medium-frequency words?

Take away

① For additional practice of joining use **PCM 6**.

② If children find any joins particularly hard, refer back to the **PCM** covering that join type in **Years 1–3**.

Warm up

🖐 Children circle shoulders forwards and backwards.

🖐 Children point fingers of both hands straight up, palms facing, then make fists. They then open their hands, with palms down and fingertips touching, make fists again, and repeat.

 **CD-ROM**

Unit focus: parallel ascenders and descenders.
Spelling link: two-syllable words containing double consonants.

Artwork
Children try to identify a word with one of the target letter patterns represented by the artwork.

Join animations
Reinforce the flowing movement in these familiar joins. Check that all ascenders are parallel and the same height; and that all descenders are parallel and the same depth.

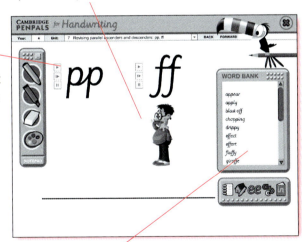

Word bank
Choose one of the words to revise parallel ascenders and descenders using the *pp, ff* and *ffe* joins. Click on the word to make the join grey for modelling and discussion. Note that in the join from *f* to *e* the cross bar of the *f* is lower than usual.

Group work

Introduce the page
● Read through the question and the list of words. Ask children to tell you which letter patterns keep cropping up on this page. Remind them of spelling work done in the past with double consonants *pp* and *ff*.

Demonstrate the unit focus
● Model tracing over the words in grey, emphasising:
  ● the fluidity of the movement
  ● the even size of the letters
  ● the parallel ascenders and descenders.
● Discuss the relative heights of the cross bar on *toffee* and *truffle*.
● Put a tick next to all the things that are edible.

  Show Me Children practise writing some of the words, keeping ascenders and descenders parallel.

● Can the children suggest other words featuring the letter patterns *pp* or *ff*? (e.g. *happy, puppy, offer, different*)

  Show Me Children practise writing these words too.

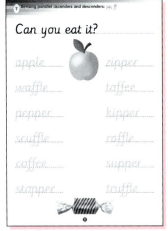

Big Book page 8

Independent work

Watch while children copy the joins. ❶

Encourage the children to read the rubric and ❷ to read through the words before they begin the activity. Encourage them to sort the words into alphabetical order in rough before copying them out neatly. Check that the ascenders and descenders are parallel on the words they write.

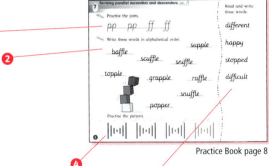

Practice Book page 8

Encourage children to practise the pattern in the bottom panel.

  Can the children look, say, cover, write and check these medium-frequency words?

Take away

① For additional practice of joining use **PCM 7**.

② If children find any joins particularly hard, refer back to the **PCM** covering that join type in **Years 1–3**.

Warm up

👋 Children lift one shoulder to their ear, then the other.

👋 Ask the children to make both their hands as wide and flat as they can and then to press their hands down hard on the table in front of them. Let them push as hard as they can for five seconds, then have a five-second break, before pushing down again for ten seconds.

CD-ROM

Unit focus: revising joins to an anticlockwise letter.
Spelling link: two-syllable words containing double consonants.

Artwork
Children try to identify a word with one of the target letter patterns represented by the artwork.

Join animations
Reinforce the flowing movement in these familiar joins. Check that ascenders are parallel and the same height. Check that both letters are correctly formed each time.

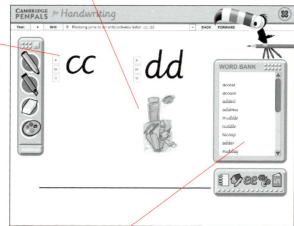

Word bank
Choose one of the words to revise joins to an anticlockwise letter using the *cc* and *dd* joins. Click on the word to make the join grey for modelling and discussion.

Group work

Introduce the page
● Read through the police report. Can children spot which letter patterns they're going to be practising this time? Remind them of the anticlockwise letters (see joining letter sets, inside back cover).

Demonstrate the unit focus
● Model tracing over the words in grey, giving particular emphasis to the fluidity of the movement on the joins to anticlockwise letters (mostly *cc, dd*).

Show Me Children practise writing the words. Remind children to keep the ascenders parallel, even though they're concentrating on the anticlockwise letters too.

● Can the children suggest other words featuring the letter patterns *cc* or *dd*? (e.g. *broccoli, accept, muddle, adding*)

Show Me Children practise writing these words too.

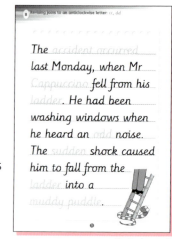
Big Book page 9

Independent work

Watch while children copy the joins. **1**

Encourage the children to read the rubric. **2** Check their hand moves across the page fluently as they write, and that on the double consonants they finish forming one letter correctly before they write the second. Look out for parallel ascenders and descenders too.

Encourage children to practise the pattern in the bottom panel. **4**

Can the children look, say, cover, write and check these words? **3**

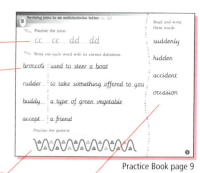
Practice Book page 9

Take away

① For additional practice of joining use **PCM 8**.

② If children find any joins particularly hard, refer back to the **PCM** covering that join type in **Years 1–3**.

9 Revising break letters: alphabetical order

Warm up

✋ Children cross their arms, raise them up high, then shake them out.
✋ Children clasp their hands together, press their palms together, then spread their fingers wide.

CD-ROM

Unit focus: revising break letters.
Vocabulary link: to sequence words in alphabetical order.

Artwork
Children try to identify a word with the target letter pattern represented by the artwork.

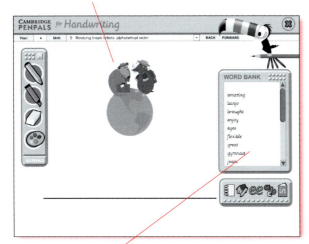

Word bank
Choose one of the words to revise break letters. Click on the word to make the break letters grey for modelling and discussion.

Group work

Introduce the page
- Look at the break letters at the top of the page. Remind the children that we don't join from *g*, *j* and *y*, and that we don't join either to or from *x* and *z*.
- Read the names and then ask which ones describe shapes.

Demonstrate the unit focus
- Model tracing over the words in grey, emphasising the fact that no joins are made from the break letters (and that *x* and *z* are not joined to either).
- As you work through the items, discuss which are real words for shapes and which are made-up ones. (*polygon, pentangle, hexagon, triangle, zigzag* are real words)
  Show Me Children practise writing the words.
- Can the children suggest other shape words featuring the break letters? (e.g. *rectangle, pentagon, heptagon, octagon, pyramid, cylinder, polyhedron*)
  Show Me Children practise writing these words too.
- Discuss how to put the words in alphabetical order. (either copy them out again on a whiteboard, or number the words on the Big Book page)

Big Book page 10

Independent work

Watch while children copy the letters. Point out that they're in alphabetical order. ❶

Encourage the children to read the rubric and the text (helping them with the word *zygodactyl* if necessary!). Check that they are joining all the letters except the break letters. ❷

Encourage children to practise the pattern in the bottom panel. ❹

Can the children look, say, cover, write and check these medium-frequency words? ❸

Practice Book page 10

Take away

① For additional practice of words with break letters use **PCM 9**.
② If children need further practice, refer back to **Year 2 PCM 2**.

Warm up

🖐 Children make large circling movements with their arms outstretched.
🖐 Children make smaller circling movements with their arms close to their bodies.

CD-ROM

Unit focus: linking spelling and handwriting.
Spelling link: to build related words with similar patterns.

Artwork
Children try to identify a word represented by the artwork and a word related to it.

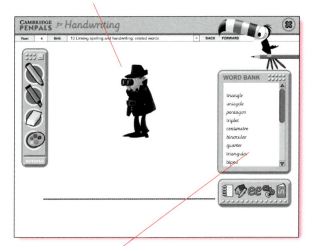

Word bank
Choose one of the words to practise handwriting by linking to spelling. Click on the word to make it grey for modelling and discussion. Ask children to find a related word in the word bank. Discuss how the meanings of the words differ.

Group work

Introduce the page
● Explain that in this unit you are going practise writing words that are related, and that share similar patterns. Point out that recognising patterns in words can help with spelling.

Demonstrate the unit focus
● Look at the words *television* and *reality*. Point out how each word has different elements: how would the children split *television*? (*tele + vision*) How about *reality*? (*real + ity*)
● Divide the class into pairs. Each pair should race to make a chain of six words, starting with one of the words at the top of the page. Each new word in a word chain must link to the word before by sharing one of the elements. Demonstrate with an example using other words (e.g. *music → musician → musical → comical → comedy → comic*). The children should write the words in their word chain on their whiteboards.
● Once they have completed the task, model writing some of their words in the spaces provided.
● Ask children to suggest different words to begin the word chains and play the game again.

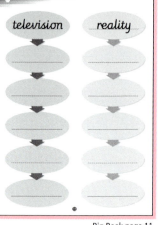

Big Book page 11

Independent work

Watch while children copy the heading. **1**

Make sure children understand the aim of the activity – to make **2** word chains linking words with similar elements. If any children are confused about where to start, suggest *microscope, medic* and *comic* as possible starting points. Three possible answers are (*microscope → microphone → telephone → telescope → television; medic → medicine → medical → musical → music → musician → electrician → electric → electrical; comic → comical → comedian → comedy → tragedy → tragic*) although, of course, these are not the only options.

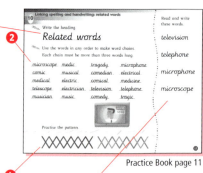

Practice Book page 11

Encourage children to practise the pattern in the bottom panel.

Can the children look, say, cover, write and check these words? **3**

Take away

① For additional joining practice use **PCM 10**.
② If children find any joins particularly hard, refer back to the **PCM** covering that join type in **Years 1–3**.

11 Introducing sloped writing

NB: the lined PCM on page 64 is designed to help children achieve an even slope in their writing.

NB: the lined PCM on page 64 is designed to help children achieve an even slope in their writing.

Warm up

- ✋ Children circle shoulders forwards and backwards.
- ✋ Children point the fingers of both hands straight up, palms facing, then make fists. They then open their hands, with palms down and fingertips touching, make fists again and repeat.

CD-ROM

Unit focus: introducing sloped writing.
Spelling link: to practise new spellings by using Look, Say, Cover, Write, Check.

Artwork
Children try to identify a word represented by the artwork.

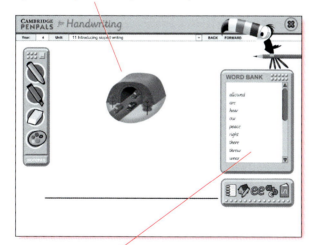

Word bank
Choose one of the words to introduce sloped writing. Click on the word to make it grey for modelling and discussion. Ask children to find a word in the word bank that sounds the same. Discuss spelling differences.

Group work

Introduce the page
- Explain that children are going to learn to slope their writing to help them to write more smoothly and quickly. Read and enjoy the jokes.

Demonstrate the unit focus
- Look at the joke in upright font and compare it with the joke in sloping font. Point out that all the things children have learned about joined writing still apply (e.g. diagonal and horizontal joins, break letters, parallel ascenders and descenders, even size and spacing).
- Can children see that the writing slopes slightly to the right? (The red lines emphasise this.)

  Get Up and Go Ask children to add sloped lines to the letters with ascenders and descenders.

- Model tracing over the words in grey. Emphasise the fact that all the letters slope at the same angle (including capitals), and that it's just a very slight slope.

  Show Me Children copy out selected words. They can practise writing any tricky words from the Big Book on a separate piece of paper, to learn later.

Big Book page 12

Independent work

Watch while children copy the heading. **1**

Emphasise that it's especially important to sit **2** correctly when you're doing sloped writing. Correct any postural and paper-positioning problems and watch while children copy the poem, making sure that they don't exaggerate the slope too much and encouraging them to keep the slope even.

Encourage children to practise the pattern in the bottom panel.

Can the children look, say, cover, write and check these medium-frequency words?

Practice Book page 12

Take away

For additional practice of sloped writing use **PCM 11**.

12 Parallel ascenders: *al*, *ad*, *af*

Warm up

- 👆 Ask the children to put their hands on their laps. When you say 'quick' they should lift their hands as high as they can and as quickly as they can. When you say 'slow' they should move their hands as slowly as possible, but with great control. Let them practise raising and lowering their hands and arms as you say 'quick' and 'slow'.
- 👆 Children repeat the above activity with just their fingers.

CD-ROM

Unit focus: practising parallel ascenders in sloped writing.
Spelling link: prefixes **al**, **ad**, **af**.

Artwork

Children try to identify a word with one of the target letter patterns represented by the artwork.

Join animations

Check that the children recognise these letter patterns as prefixes. Point out that the letters are consistently sloped.

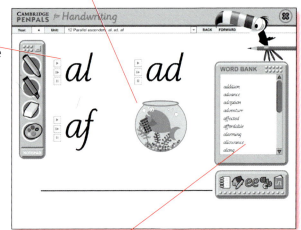

Word bank

Choose one of the words to practise parallel ascenders using the prefixes *al*, *ad* and *af*. Click on the word to make the join grey for modelling and discussion.

Group work

Introduce the page

- Read through the words in the box and explain that you are going to be sorting them into adjectives and adverbs, focusing on *al*, *ad*, *af*. (Make sure children remember what adjectives and adverbs are.)

Demonstrate the unit focus

- Read each word from the box aloud and ask children to tell you whether it is an adverb or an adjective. If necessary, remind children that adverbs often end in *ly*. They can also test which category a word belongs to by trying it out in front of a noun (adjective) or a verb (adverb).
- Model writing the words up in the correct column. Emphasise the fact that the ascenders are still parallel even though the writing is sloped.
  Show Me Children write the words. Check that the ascenders are parallel.
- Can children think of any other words beginning with *al*, *ad* and *af*? (e.g. *almighty*, *admit*, *affect*) Model writing these up.
  Show Me Children practise writing these words too.

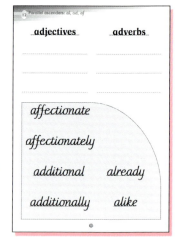

Independent work

Watch while children practise the joins. **1**

Watch while children write the words, **2** ensuring they choose the correct letter pattern. Check that they keep their ascenders parallel.

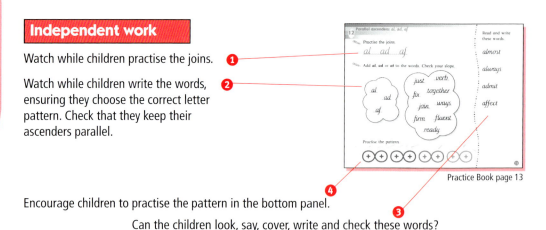

Practice Book page 13

Encourage children to practise the pattern in the bottom panel. **4**

Can the children look, say, cover, write and check these words? **3**

Take away

For additional practice of parallel ascenders in sloped writing use **PCM 12**.

13 Parallel descenders and break letters: *ight, ough*

Warm up

- ✋ Children put their arm straight up in the air, bend the elbow so the hand is on the back of the neck, then gently push the front of the elbow with the opposite hand.
- ✋ Ask the children to press fingertips of the fingers on each hand together. Can they press them together hard for ten seconds? For the next ten seconds, keeping their fingertips together, they can gently bounce their fingers, before pressing them hard again for another ten seconds.

CD-ROM

Unit focus: practising parallel descenders in sloped writing.
Spelling link: common endings **ight**, **ough**.

Artwork
Children try to identify a word with one of the target letter patterns represented by the artwork.

Join animations
Check that the children know how to pronounce these letter patterns. Point out that the letters are consistently sloped.

Word bank
Choose one of the words to practise parallel descenders and break letters using the letter patterns *ight* and *ough*. Click on the word to make the letter pattern grey for modelling and discussion.

Group work

Introduce the page
- Read through the facts on the page. Can children guess why some words are in grey? Focus on *ight*, *ough* as spelling patterns. Remind the children of spelling work done in the past.

Demonstrate the unit focus
- Model tracing over the words in grey, emphasising the fact that the descenders are parallel in words like *flight* and *frightened*. If necessary, draw faint lines on the text to emphasise the slope.
  Show Me Children write the words. Check that their descenders are parallel.
- Can children think of any other words ending with *ight* and *ough*? (e.g. *bright, tight, rough, tough*) Model writing these up.
  Show Me Children practise writing these words too.

Big Book page 14

Independent work

Watch while children practise the joins. **①**

Watch while children write the words, **②** ensuring they get the spellings correct. Check that they keep the descenders parallel. (The answers are *light / bright, right, cough, dough, night, fright, through, thought / bright*).

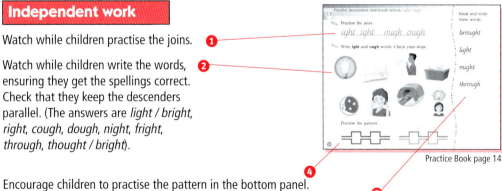
Practice Book page 14

Encourage children to practise the pattern in the bottom panel.

Can the children look, say, cover, write and check these medium-frequency words?

Take away

For additional practice of parallel descenders in sloped writing use **PCM 13**.

Warm up

- Children lift one shoulder to their ear, then the other.
- Ask the children to make both their hands as wide and flat as they can and then to press their hands down hard on the table in front of them. Let them push as hard as they can for five seconds, then have a five-second break, before pushing down again for ten seconds.

CD-ROM

Unit focus: practising size, proportion and spacing in sloped writing.

Spelling link: words ending **ious**.

Artwork

Children try to identify a word with the target letter pattern represented by the artwork.

Join animation

Check that the children know how to pronounce this letter pattern. Point out that the letters are consistently sloped.

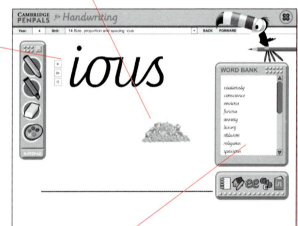

Word bank

Choose one of the words that includes *ious* to practise size, proportion and spacing. Click on the word to make the joins grey for modelling and discussion. Ask children to find a related word in the word bank.

Group work

Introduce the page

- Read through the text and ask children what all the grey words have in common. (They end in *ious*.) Remind children of spelling work done in the past.

Demonstrate the unit focus

- Model tracing over the words in grey with an even, fluid movement. Emphasise the slight slope to the right, and the fact that all the letters slope at the same angle. If necessary, draw lines on the text to emphasise the slope.

  Show Me Children write the words. Check the size, proportion and spacing of their writing.

- Can children think of any other words ending in *ious*? (e.g. *vicious, obvious, precious*) Model writing these up.

  Show Me Children practise writing these words too.

Big Book page 15

Independent work

Watch while children practise the joins. **1**

Encourage children to read through the words **2** in each column. Help with definitions of words they don't understand. Watch while they write the pairs of words, checking the size, proportion and spacing of the words are correct.

Practice Book page 15

Encourage children to practise the pattern in the bottom panel.

Can the children look, say, cover, write and check these words?

Take away

For additional practice of size, proportion and spacing in sloped writing use **PCM 14**.

15 Size, proportion and spacing: *able, ful*

Warm up

👋 Children shake out their arms.

👋 Children shake out their hands, letting their fingers flop loosely.

CD-ROM

Unit focus: practising size, proportion and spacing in sloped writing.

Vocabulary link: suffixes **able**, **ful**.

Artwork

Children try to identify a word with one of the target letter patterns represented by the artwork.

Join animations

Check that the children know these are suffixes. Check that the size, proportion and spacing of the letters are consistent.

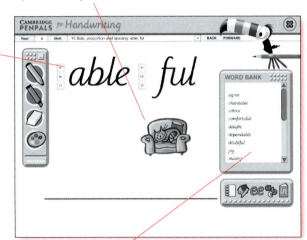

Word bank

Choose one of the words that includes *able* or *ful* to practise size, proportion and spacing. Click on the word to make the joins grey for modelling and discussion. Ask children to find a related word in the word bank.

Group work

Introduce the page

● Read through the poster, explaining that it's an advert for a new kind of collectable toy. Remind children you can make adjectives by adding the suffixes *able* and *ful* to nouns and verbs.

Demonstrate the unit focus

● Model tracing over the words in grey with an even, fluid movement. Emphasise the slight slope to the right, and the fact that all the letters slope at the same angle.

● Point out that 'NEW GNOMES' is written in upright capitals. Sloped capitals are likely only to be used in fluent writing.

  Show Me Children write some of the words. Check the size, proportion and spacing of their writing.

● Can children think of any other words ending with *able* and *ful*? (e.g. *washable, changeable, wonderful, beautiful*) Model writing these up.

  Show Me Children practise writing these words too.

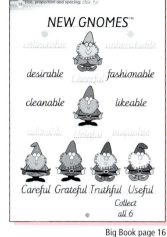

Big Book page 16

Independent work

Watch while children practise the joins. **1**

Watch while children write the words, **2** reminding them if necessary of the spelling rule that means *y* changes to *i* and *e* is dropped when adding *able*. Check the slope, size, proportion and spacing of their writing.

Practice Book page 16

Encourage children to practise the pattern in the bottom panel.

Can the children look, say, cover, write and check these words?

Take away

For additional practice of size, proportion and spacing in sloped writing use **PCM 15**.

31

Warm up

👆 Children tuck their chins in and roll their heads round clockwise and anticlockwise.
👆 Children clasp their hands together, press their palms together, then spread their fingers wide.

CD-ROM

Unit focus: practising size, proportion and spacing in sloped writing.
Spelling link: to add suffixes to words ending in **f**.

Artwork
Children try to identify a word with one of the target letter patterns represented by the artwork.

Join animations
Check that the children know when to use each of these word endings. Check that the size, proportion and spacing of the letters are consistent.

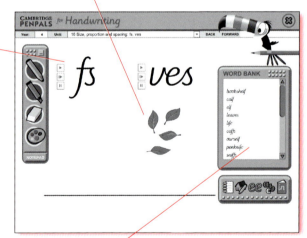

Word bank
Choose one of the words that includes *fs* or *ves* to practise size, proportion and spacing. Click on the word to make the join grey for modelling and discussion. Ask children to find a related word in the word bank.

Group work

Introduce the page
● Look at the picture and read the sentence. Explain that you are going to be practising writing the plurals of words ending with an **f** sound.

Demonstrate the unit focus
Get Up and Go Ask children to circle the words ending in *fs* or *ves* in the sentence. If any children circle *Cliff's*, use this as an opportunity to explain the difference between *s* as a plural ending and apostrophe *s* as a possessive form.

● The Big Book page has stars next to the pictures of things whose singular ends in an **f** sound. Ask children to name the items. (*knives, thieves, gloves, scarves, handkerchiefs, sugar puffs, peach halves, loaves, roofs*) Ask children to suggest how the plurals end and model writing these up in the space at the top of the artwork.
Emphasise the regularity of the slope and the even sizing and spacing of the writing.
Show Me Children write the plural forms. Check the size, proportion and spacing of their writing.

● Can children think of any other plural words ending in *fs* or *ves*? (e.g. *cuffs, muffs, wives, lives*) Model writing these up.
Show Me Children practise writing these words too.

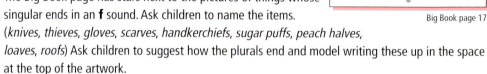

These thieves in handcuffs have taken things from Cliff's shop.

Big Book page 17

Independent work

Watch while children practise the joins. **①**

Watch while children write the words, **②** checking they choose the correct ending for the plural. Keep an eye on the size, proportion and spacing of their writing.

Practice Book page 17

Encourage children to practise the pattern in the bottom panel. **④**
③
Can the children look, say, cover, write and check these words?

Take away

For additional practice of size, proportion and spacing in sloped writing use **PCM 16**.

17 Speed and fluency: abbreviations for notes

Warm up

- Children cross their arms, raise them up high, then shake them out.
- Ask the children to make rings by touching their forefingers to their thumbs. Can they make these rings interlock? (e.g. by touching the thumb and finger of their right hand inside the ring made by the thumb and finger of their left hand) Let them make interlocking rings using each finger in turn touching their thumbs.

CD-ROM

Unit focus: practising speed and fluency in sloped writing.
Word level link: to build up speed for notes.

Artwork
Children try to identify a word represented by the artwork and think of an associated abbreviation.

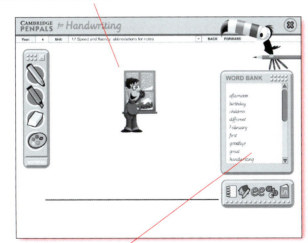

Word bank
Choose one of the words to practise speed and fluency. Click on the word to make it grey for modelling and discussion. Ask children to give an abbreviation for the word, and a situation in which you might use its abbreviated form.

Group work

Introduce the page

- Look at the words down the left-hand side of the page. Explain that you are going to look at ways of helping you write quickly, for example when you need to take notes. Discuss some of the situations in which children might need to take notes (e.g. a teacher telling them what they need to bring on a school trip, taking down a phone message, sending a text message, noting important information from a recorded message, for example cinema schedules).

Demonstrate the unit focus

- Explain that when you're noting things down quickly, you don't always need to write the whole words. You can miss some letters out or use symbols or apostrophes to help you write more quickly.
- Work your way down the list, asking children to suggest ways of abbreviating these common words.

  Show Me Children write the abbreviations.

full form	note form
and	
because	
difficult	
very	
with	
without	
thank you	
sometimes	
something	
please	

Big Book page 18

Independent work

Watch while children write the heading. **1**

Watch while children write the message in note form, encouraging children to invent their own abbreviations and to write as quickly as possible. Point out that it still has to be readable. **2**

Practice Book page 18

Encourage children to practise the pattern in the bottom panel. **4**

Can the children look, say, cover, write and check these medium-frequency words? **3**

Take away

For additional practice of abbreviations for notemaking use **PCM 17**.

Warm up

- Children point their arms up vertically above their heads, then bend their arms at the elbows, so that their hands go behind their heads.
- Children should point both their forefingers straight up vertically, bend them in the middle, then straighten them horizontally. They can repeat this movement up to five times with different fingers.

CD-ROM

Unit focus: practising speed and fluency in sloped writing.
Word level link: to build up speed for notes.

Artwork
Children try to identify a phrase represented by the artwork and think of an associated abbreviation.

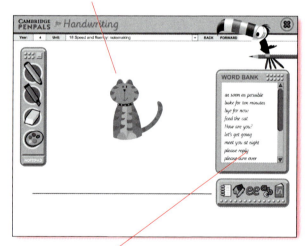

Word bank
Choose one of the phrases to practise speed and fluency. Click on the phrase to make it grey for modelling and discusssion. Ask children to say how the phrase might be abbreviated, and a situation in which you might use its abbreviated form.

Group work

Introduce the page
- Explain that you are going to practise writing quickly to make notes. Talk about the difference between informal writing, such as notes, which doesn't have to be their very best writing, and clear, neat writing which is used for other purposes, such as classwork or letter writing.

Demonstrate the unit focus
- Read through the information at the bottom of the page. Edit the text by crossing out words that aren't strictly necessary, leaving just the key facts. Recall some of the abbreviations you practised in the previous unit also.
- Model writing up notes in the form of bullet points in the space provided. For example, the final sentence could become: *most ast few m in diameter – some 160 km+.*

  Show Me Ask the children to write one of the sentences in note form by omitting words or letters. Let them talk to a partner to justify the decisions they made.

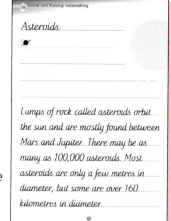

Big Book page 19

Independent work

Watch while children write the heading. **1**

Watch while children write their definition in **2** note form. Encourage them to use the abbreviations they already know, as well as inventing others themselves, and to write as quickly as possible.

Encourage children to practise the pattern in the bottom panel.

Can the children look, say, cover, write and check these medium-frequency words?

Practice Book page 19

Take away

For additional practice of notemaking use **PCM 18**.

19 Speed and fluency: drafting

Warm up

- ✋ Children alternately fold their arms then stretch them out to the sides and above their heads.
- ✋ Ask children to make fists with both their hands, then stretch their hands as wide as they will go before making fists again. They can repeat this movement several times.

CD-ROM

Unit focus: practising speed and fluency in sloped writing.
Word level link: to build up speed for drafts.

Artwork

Children try to identify an abbreviated phrase represented by the artwork and think of an associated full form.

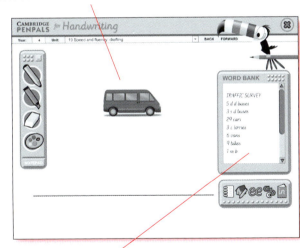

Word bank

Discuss the traffic survey results and the key at the end of the word bank. Click on a phrase to make it grey for modelling, and identify what it means. Use the notepad to write a draft of a report about the survey. Discuss the difference between note form and draft.

Group work

Introduce the page

- Explain that you are going to practise drafting texts. Ensure children understand that it's a good idea to do a first draft of any piece of writing, which you can then edit and improve upon. Explain that a draft needn't be in their very best writing, as they're going to change and improve it later on, but stress that the writing does still need to be legible!

Demonstrate the unit focus

- Read the heading and the notes on the page. Discuss how to put the facts together into a paragraph such as you might find in an information book. Explain that you'll need to add letters and words to flesh the notes out into complete words and sentences.
- Once you've agreed on a first sentence, model writing it up. Emphasise the fact that you're writing quickly and fluently, but your writing is still legible.

  Show Me Ask the children to write the second sentence themselves. Choose one of their attempts to write up, making any corrections as necessary.
- Repeat until all the bullet points have been dealt with and the paragraph is complete.

The Ichthyostega
- fish
- old waddle on land
- lived 370 m yrs ago
- 1st ancestor of dinos to live on land

Big Book page 20

Independent work

Watch while children write the heading. ❶

Watch while children write their draft paragraph, offering assistance as necessary. ❷

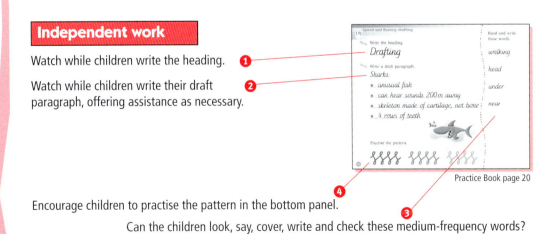

Practice Book page 20

Encourage children to practise the pattern in the bottom panel.

Can the children look, say, cover, write and check these medium-frequency words?

Take away

For additional practice of drafting use **PCM 19**.

Warm up

👋 Let children stand up, stretch their arms out in front of them and shut their eyes. Can they bring each finger in turn to touch their nose, ears or forehead?

👋 Children close their eyes and touch each finger of the opposite hand with their forefinger as fast as they can.

CD-ROM

Unit focus: practising speed and fluency in sloped writing.
Word level link: to build up speed for lists.

Artwork
Children try to identify a word represented by the artwork and the heading it might belong to.

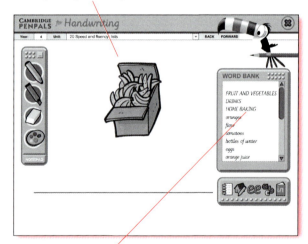

Word bank
Choose one of the three categories in capital letters. Click on the category to make it grey for modelling and discussion. On the notepad, write a list of words from the word bank that come into this category. Emphasise speed and fluency.

Group work

Introduce the page
● Explain that you are going to practise writing lists. Ask children to suggest some situations in which they might need to write lists (e.g. shopping lists, Christmas present lists, lists of equipment needed for science or PE, lists of ingredients needed for a recipe). What sort of writing is appropriate for lists? (fast and fluent)

Demonstrate the unit focus
● Read the heading in each of the boxes and the words around the edge of the page. Explain that you're going to sort the words into rivers, mountains and continents, and write each word in the appropriate list.

● Talk about the layout of a list, reminding children that each item goes on a new line, one underneath the other. Lists sometimes have headings too.

● Take suggestions from children as to which list each word should go in. If possible, have a globe or atlas on hand to help you locate the rivers, mountains and continents.

● Model writing each word in the correct list as quickly and fluently as possible.
Show Me Ask the children to try writing the lists themselves.

Big Book page 21

Independent work

Watch while children write the heading. ❶

Encourage children to read the rubric. Make sure they understand that *birds*, *plants* and *animals* are the headings for the lists. ❷
Watch while children put the words into lists, encouraging them to write as fluently as possible.

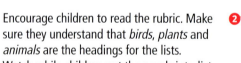

Practice Book page 21

Encourage children to practise the pattern in the bottom panel. ❹ ❸
Can the children look, say, cover, write and check these medium-frequency words?

Take away

For additional practice of making lists use **PCM 20**.

21 Size, proportion and spacing: ν, k

Warm up

✋ Children make large circling movements with their arms outstretched.
✋ Children make smaller circling movements with their arms close to their bodies.

CD-ROM

Unit focus: practising size, proportion and spacing in sloped writing.
Spelling link: to explore the occurrence of **v** and **k**.

Artwork
Children try to identify a word with one of the target letter patterns represented by the artwork.

Letter animations
What do children know about when and how often the letters ν and k are used? What common spelling patterns are they part of? (e.g. *ve* and *ck*)? Check the size and proportion of the letters.

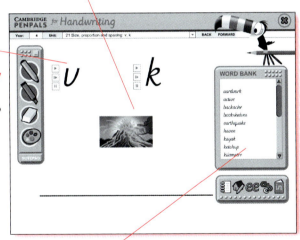

Word bank
Choose one of the words to practise size, proportion and spacing using the letters ν and k. Click on the word to make the letters ν and k grey for modelling and discussion.

Group work

Introduce the page
● Read through the text and ask children to spot which letters occur frequently. (ν and k) Remind children of spelling work done in the past.

Demonstrate the unit focus
Get Up and Go Ask children to come up and circle words containing the letters ν and k.

● Model tracing over the sentence in grey, emphasising the even size of the letters, the correct proportion between short letters and letters with ascenders and descenders, and the equal spacing.

Show Me Ask the children to try writing some of the words themselves.

● Can children suggest any other words with ν or k at the beginning, in the middle or at the end? Model writing these up.

Show Me Children try writing these words too.

> *I've never seen anything like it*
> *As the lava flowed from the*
> *volcano, I saw crackling sparks*
> *of violet, pink and black. The*
> *ground chucked out thick,*
> *stinking smoke and I cried,*
> *"Let's evacuate, or we'll all be*
> *killed!"*

Big Book page 22

Independent work

Watch while children practise the joins. **1**

Encourage children to read the rubric and to read through the words and definitions before they begin. Watch while they copy the words, ensuring that the spacing, size and proportion of the letters are correct. **2**

Encourage children to practise the pattern in the bottom panel.

Can the children look, say, cover, write and check these medium-frequency words?

Practice Book page 22

3 4

Take away

For additional practice of size, proportion and spacing use **PCM 21**.

Warm up

✋ Children tuck their chins in and roll their heads round clockwise and anticlockwise.

✋ Children rotate their wrists clockwise and anticlockwise.

CD-ROM

Unit focus: practising size, proportion and spacing in sloped writing.

Spelling link: suffixes **ic** and **ist**.

Artwork

Children try to identify a word with one of the target letter patterns represented by the artwork.

Join animations

What do the children know about these suffixes? Do they know spelling rules for applying them? Check that the size, proportion and spacing of the letters are consistent.

Word bank

Choose one of the words that includes the suffix *ic* or *ist* to practise size, proportion and spacing. Click on the word to make the join grey for modelling and discussion. Discuss how the suffixes can be used with other words in the word bank.

Group work

Introduce the page

● Read through the suffixes and the root words on the page. Explain that you're going to practise writing extended words, by adding the suffixes *ic* and *ist* to root words. Can children see that adding *ist* gives you the noun for a person who does something, and adding *ic* gives you an adjective?

Demonstrate the unit focus

● Model tracing over the words in grey, emphasising the even size of the letters, the correct proportion between short letters and letters with ascenders and descenders, and the equal spacing. Discuss spelling changes as appropriate for your class.

● Ask children to tell you what happens when you add *ist* to *art*. (you get *artist*) Model writing this word up. What about when you then add *ic*? (*artistic*) Model this word too.

Show Me Children try writing the words themselves.

● Repeat with the remaining words, talking through any spelling changes as appropriate for your class.

● Can children suggest any other words ending in *ic* or *ist*? (e.g. *allergic, energetic, specialist, stockist*) Model writing these up.

Show Me Children practise writing these words too.

Big Book page 23

Independent work

Watch while children practise the joins. **①**

Encourage children to read the rubric and to read through the words before they begin. Watch while they copy the words, ensuring that the spacing, size and proportion of the letters are correct. **②**

Encourage children to practise the pattern in the bottom panel. **④**

Can the children look, say, cover, write and check these medium-frequency words? **③**

Practice Book page 23

Take away

For additional practice of size, proportion and spacing use **PCM 22**.

Warm up

👆 Children circle shoulders forwards and backwards.

👆 Children point fingers of both hands straight up, palms facing, then make fists. They then open their hands, with palms down and fingertips touching, make fists again and repeat.

 **CD-ROM**

Unit focus: practising size, proportion and spacing in sloped writing.

Spelling link: suffixes **sion** and **tion**.

Artwork
Children try to identify a word with the target letter pattern represented by the artwork.

Join animation
What do the children know about this suffix? Do they know spelling rules for applying it? Check that the size, proportion and spacing of the letters are consistent.

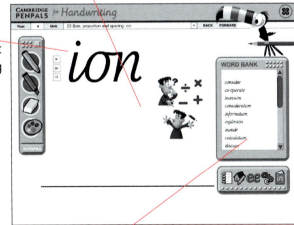

Word bank
Choose one of the words that includes the suffix *ion* to practise size, proportion and spacing. Click on the word to make the join grey for modelling and discussion. Discuss how the suffix can be used with other words in the word bank.

Group work

Introduce the page
● Explain that you're going to be practising writing nouns that come from verbs. Remind children of spelling work on *ion* done in the past.

Demonstrate the unit focus
● Model tracing over the word *decision*, emphasising the even size of the letters, the correct proportion between short letters and letters with ascenders, and the equal spacing.

● Discuss how you need to modify the spelling when adding *ion* to *decide*.

Show Me Children try writing the word themselves.

● Repeat with the remaining words, talking through any spelling changes as appropriate for your class.

● Can children suggest any other words ending in *ion*? (e.g. *addition*, *multiplication*, *revision*, *division*) Model writing these up.

Show Me Children practise writing these words too.

verb	noun
decide	*decision*
vary	
educate	
confuse	
punctuate	
extend	
create	
conclude	
expect	

Big Book page 24

Independent work

Watch while children practise the joins. ❶

Encourage children to read the rubric and to read through the text before they begin. Watch while they copy the sentences, ensuring that the size, proportion and spacing of the letters are correct. ❷

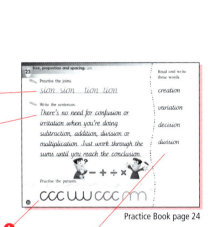

Practice Book page 24

Encourage children to practise the pattern in the bottom panel. ❹

Can the children look, say, cover, write and check these words? ❸

Take away

For additional practice of size, proportion and spacing use **PCM 23**.

Warm up

- Children lift one shoulder to their ear, then the other.
- Ask the children to make both their hands as wide and flat as they can and then to press their hands down hard on the table in front of them. Let them push as hard as they can for five seconds, then have a five-second break, before pushing down again for ten seconds.

CD-ROM

Unit focus: practising size, proportion and spacing in sloped writing.

Spelling link: to distinguish *its* and *it's*.

Artwork

Children try to identify a phrase and its contracted form represented by the artwork.

Join animations

Do the children know how to tell these two words apart? Discuss strategies. Check that the size, proportion and spacing of the letters are consistent.

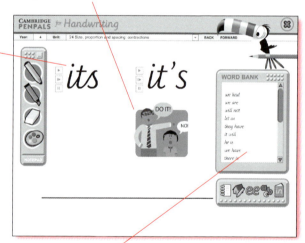

Word bank

Choose one of the phrases to practise size, proportion and spacing. Click on the phrase to make it grey for modelling and discussion. Ask children to use the notepad to write its contracted form.

Group work

Introduce the page

- Read through the text and underline all instances of *its* and *it's*. Discuss the difference at a level appropriate for your class.

Demonstrate the unit focus

Get Up and Go Ask children to come up and circle all the words meaning 'belonging to it' (i.e. *its*).

- Model tracing over these words, concentrating on the relative size of the letters and the spacing.

Show Me Children practise writing the word themselves.

Get Up and Go Ask children to come up and circle all the contractions of 'it is' (i.e. *it's*).

- Model tracing over these words, concentrating on the relative size of the letters and the spacing, especially around the apostrophe.

Show Me Children practise writing the word themselves.

The Grumpy Ladybird

The ladybird was just finishing its lunch of greenflies. "It's not fair," it sighed. "Look at that other ladybird, standing on its own leaf and eating its own supply of greenfly. It's not inviting me to share its feast. No, it's not fair. It's definitely not fair."

Big Book page 25

Independent work

Watch while children practise the joins. **①**

Encourage children to read the rubric. Watch while they copy the sentences, ensuring that they choose the correct word each time and that the spacing, size and proportion of the letters are correct. **②**

Practice Book page 25

Encourage children to practise the pattern in the bottom panel. **④**

Can the children look, say, cover, write and check these medium-frequency words? **③**

Take away

For additional practice of size, proportion and spacing use **PCM 24.**

Warm up

👋 Ask the children to put their hands on their laps. When you say 'quick' they should lift their hands as high as they can and as quickly as they can. When you say 'slow' they should move their hands as slowly as possible, but with great control. Let them practise raising and lowering their hands and arms as you say 'quick' and 'slow'.

👋 Children repeat the above activity with just their fingers.

CD-ROM

Unit focus: practising speed and fluency in sloped writing.
Spelling link: suffixes **ible** and **able**.

Artwork
Children try to identify a word with one of the target letter patterns represented by the artwork.

Join animations
Do the children know any words ending with these suffixes? Do they know spelling rules for adding them to words? Check that the size, proportion and spacing of the letters are consistent.

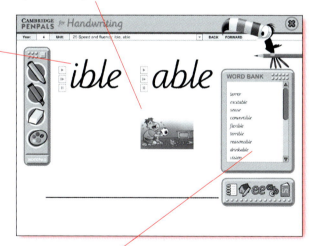

Word bank
Choose one of the words that includes the suffix *ible* or *able* to practise speed and fluency. Click on the word to make the join grey for modelling and discussion. Discuss how the suffix can be used with other words in the word bank.

Group work

Introduce the page
● Read through the text and explain that you're going to practise writing words with the endings *ible* and *able*, choosing the correct ending each time.

Demonstrate the unit focus
● Ask children to suggest the correct ending for the first word in grey (*miserable*). Model tracing over the word and adding the correct ending, concentrating on the swift and flowing movement of your writing.

   Show Me Children practise writing the word themselves.
● Repeat with the other words.
● Ask if children can suggest any other words ending in *ible* and *able*. (e.g. *terrible, edible, washable, readable*) Model writing these up.

   Show Me Children practise writing these words too.

Big Book page 26

Independent work

Watch while children practise the joins. ❶

Encourage children to read the rubric. ❷
Watch while they copy the pairs of words, ensuring that they are writing with a fluent movement and encouraging them to try speeding up their writing as they progress through the task.

Practice Book page 26

Encourage children to practise the pattern in the bottom panel. ❸ ❹

   Can the children look, say, cover, write and check these words?

Take away

For additional practice of speed and fluency use **PCM 25**.

Warm up

- ✋ Children put their arm straight up in the air, bend the elbow so the hand is on the back of the neck, then gently push the front of the elbow with the opposite hand.
- ✋ Ask the children to press fingertips of the fingers on each hand together. Can they press them together hard for ten seconds? For the next ten seconds, keeping their fingertips together, they can gently bounce their fingers, before pressing them hard again for another ten seconds.

CD-ROM

Unit focus: practising speed and fluency in sloped writing.
Vocabulary link: diminutives.

Artwork

Children try to identify a word and its diminutive represented by the artwork.

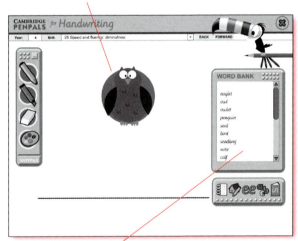

Word bank

Choose one of the words to practise speed and fluency. Click on the word to make it grey for modelling and discussion. Ask children to find a related word in the word bank.

Group work

Introduce the page

- Ensure that children understand what diminutives are (words which imply smallness). If appropriate, discuss some ways of making diminutives (suffixes *let*, *ette*, *ling*; prefixes *mini*, *micro*). Read through the text and explain that you're going to practise speeding up your writing.

Demonstrate the unit focus

Get Up and Go Ask children to come up and circle any words that are diminutives (*minibus, ducklings, goslings, saplings, kitchenette, minibeasts*; you may also wish to look at the words *weaklings, microscope*).

- To get across the idea of increased speed and fluency in writing, trace over the text in grey, emphasising the rapid and flowing movement of your hand.

Show Me Children practise writing one or two words themselves.

- Ask if children can suggest any other diminutives. (e.g. *leaflet, usherette, miniskirt*) Model writing these up.

Show Me Children practise writing these words too.

Last week we visited a city farm. We went in the school minibus. There's a pond with ducklings and goslings, and a forest of saplings. They look like weaklings now, but they'll be huge one day. There is also a kitchenette where the animals' meals are made. The best bit was looking at some minibeasts under a microscope!

Big Book page 27

Independent work

Watch while children practise the joins. **1**

Encourage children to read the rubric. **2** Watch while they write out the diminutive words, ensuring that they are writing with a flowing movement and encouraging them to try speeding up their writing as they progress through the task.

Encourage children to practise the pattern in the bottom panel.

Can the children look, say, cover, write and check these words?

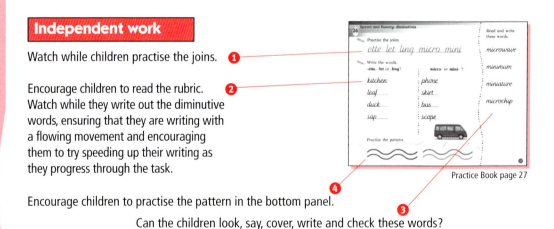

Practice Book page 27

Take away

For additional practice of speed and fluency use **PCM 26**.

Warm up

- Children shake out their arms.
- Children shake out their hands, letting their fingers flop loosely.

CD-ROM

Unit focus: print alphabet.
Word level link: presentational skills.

Artwork

Children try to identify which words are needed to label the volcano on the artwork.

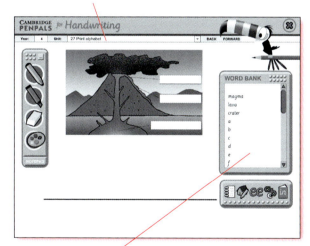

Word bank

Choose a letter to practise lower case letters in the print alphabet. Click on a letter to make it grey for modelling and discussion. Can the children identify what makes the print alphabet different from handwriting? Identify where the three labels in the word bank belong on the diagram.

Group work

Introduce the page

- Read through the page and explain that it comes from a pupil's geography exercise book. Look at the two different types of writing used and identify the fact that print is used for the labels. Discuss the reasons for this (to make sure that this important text is clear). Discuss ways of making headings stand out (e.g. colour, size, underlining).

Demonstrate the unit focus

- Model tracing over the words in grey, reminding children of the formation of the letters in print font. Note that you don't put flicks on the letters when you are printing.

  Show Me Children practise writing these words themselves.

- Ask children to suggest a heading and a caption for the picture and write them up in print lettering.

  Show Me Children practise writing the heading and caption themselves.

Big Book page 28

Independent work

Watch while children write out the heading, labels and caption, ensuring that they use print rather than joined writing.

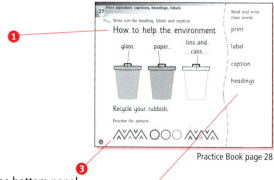

Practice Book page 28

Encourage children to practise the pattern in the bottom panel.

Can the children look, say, cover, write and check these medium-frequency words?

Take away

For additional practice of the print alphabet use **PCM 27**.

NB: for a purpose such as a poster, children will be more likely to use upright print capitals. Sloped capitals are only likely to be used as part of continuous sloped handwriting.

Warm up

- Children cross their arms, raise them up high, then shake them out.
- Children clasp their hands together, press their palms together, then spread their fingers wide.

CD-ROM

Unit focus: print capitals.
Word level link: presentational skills.

Artwork
Children try to identify letters to make a label to represent the artwork.

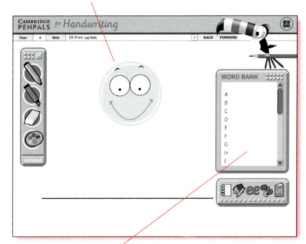

Word bank
Choose a letter to practise capital letters in the print alphabet. Click on a letter to make it grey for modelling and discussion. On the notepad, try writing names and labels for classroom equipment in capital print letters.

Group work

Introduce the page
- Read through the poster. Ask children why they think print capitals have been used. (They make the poster clear and easy to read, even from a distance.) Remind children about the basic formation of capitals (top to bottom, left to right).

Demonstrate the unit focus
- Model tracing over the words in grey, reminding children of the formation of the capitals.

  Show Me Children practise writing these words themselves.
- Ask children why they think 'See you there!' isn't written in print font. (It's not vital information.)

Big Book page 29

Independent work

Watch while children copy out the poster, ensuring that they use print capitals. If any children finish early, they can write out the whole alphabet in capitals.

Practice Book page 29

Encourage children to practise the pattern in the bottom panel.

Can the children look, say, cover, write and check these medium-frequency words?

Take away

For additional practice of print capitals use **PCM 28**.

NB: the Big Book pages in this unit offer an opportunity to consolidate the work covered this year. The results of children's Practice Book work can be used as an end-of-year assessment to measure their progress and identify targets for the coming year.

Warm up

👆 Children tuck their chins in and roll their heads clockwise and anticlockwise.

👆 Ask the children to make rings by touching their forefingers to their thumbs. Can they make these rings interlock? (e.g. by touching the thumb and finger of their right hand inside the ring made by the thumb and finger of their left hand) Let them make interlocking rings using each finger in turn touching their thumbs.

CD-ROM

Unit focus: consolidating and assessing all work from Year 4.
Word level link: to use joined handwriting for all writing except where other special forms are required.

Sample of handwriting
The children use PCM 29 to assess the handwriting sample. They then use the same PCM to complete a self-assessment of a recent piece of their own writing.

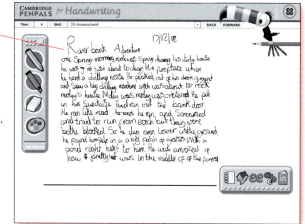

Group work

Introduce the page
● Explain to children that this unit will give them a chance to recap what they have learnt this year, and to see how good their handwriting is.

Demonstrate the unit focus
● Read through the text on the left-hand page together. Talk about the layout, including the print capital letters for the main heading, the print font for subheadings and the joined font for main text.

● Read the bulleted list on the right-hand page. Tell the children that these are useful things to think about whenever they have to copy a passage.

● Talk about each of the issues in turn.

● As children identify any words they think they might find tricky, model tracing over them.

   Show Me Children practise writing these words themselves.

● Pick up on any other issues as appropriate to your class and demonstrate these once again.

THE PLANET MARS

The red planet
The planet's surface is rich in rusted iron, which is why it looks red.
Temperature
The surface temperature ranges from 26°C during the day, to as low as −110°C at night.
Water
There is no liquid water on Mars, but ice has been found at the poles.

Big Book page 30

Independent work

Watch while children copy ❶ out the text.

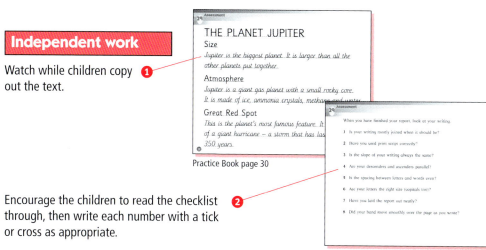

THE PLANET JUPITER
Size
Jupiter is the biggest planet. It is larger than all the other planets put together.
Atmosphere
Jupiter is a giant gas planet with a small rocky core. It is made of ice, ammonia crystals, methane and water.
Great Red Spot
This is the planet's most famous feature. It of a giant hurricane – a storm that has las 350 years.

Practice Book page 30

Encourage the children to read the checklist ❷ through, then write each number with a tick or cross as appropriate.

When you have finished your report, look at your writing.
1 Is your writing mostly joined when it should be?
2 Have you used print script correctly?
3 Is the slope of your writing always the same?
4 Are your descenders and ascenders parallel?
5 Is the spacing between letters and words even?
6 Are your letters the right size (capitals too)?
7 Have you laid the report out neatly?
8 Did your hand move smoothly over the page as you wrote?

Practice Book page 31

Take away

An opportunity for self-assessment is provided on **PCM 29**.

30 Presentational skills

NB: this unit is intended as a relatively light-hearted end to the handwriting year, following the assessment in Unit 29.

Warm up

 Children point their arms up vertically above their heads, then bend their arms at the elbows, so that their hands go behind their heads.

 Children should point both their forefingers straight up vertically, bend them in the middle, then straighten them horizontally. They can repeat this movement up to five times with different fingers.

CD-ROM

Unit focus: presentational skills.
Word level link: to use a range of fonts.

Font styles

Discuss the four different font styles of the capital letter A. Model writing the letters and then ask the children to practise writing their initials in the style of these capital letters.

Group work

Introduce the page

- Read the extracts through. Explain that we can use a variety of different font styles, both computer generated and handwritten, to make texts more interesting to look at. However, we need to think carefully about whether our chosen font is suitable for the type of text we're writing.

Demonstrate the unit focus

- Discuss the different fonts used for the extracts, discussing the suitability of each for the content.
- Where do the children think the first extract comes from? (a newspaper headline) Why is a bold capital font used? (so the text stands out and is clear and easy to read)
- Look at the second extract. How would children describe this font? (old-fashioned) Why do they think this font is suitable for the text? (it's about times past)
- Repeat this discussion process for the remaining two texts (an extract from a computer instruction book and a joke).

  Show Me Children can practise copying words in the different font styles.

CITY AND UNITED SIGN TRANSFER DEAL

In 1666, London burned like rotten sticks.

First switch on the modem then click on the Internet icon.

What do you get if you cross a skeleton with a tumble drier? Bone dry clothes.

Big Book page 32

Independent work

Watch while children copy the heading. **1**

Encourage the children to read the rubric. **2** Watch while they write the extracts, first in their normal handwriting, then in a more interesting way.

Encourage children to practise the pattern in the bottom panel. **4**

Can the children look, say, cover, write and check these medium-frequency words? **3**

Presentational skills 30

Write the heading
Writing styles

Copy the joke in two different styles.
What do you get if you cross a cow with a jogging machine?
A milk shake!

Practise the pattern

Read and write these words.
today
asked
friends
upon

Practice Book page 32

Take away

For additional practice of writing styles use **PCM 30**.

UNIT 1 Revising joins in a word: *ness, ship*

1

Name .... Date ....

Practise the joins. *ness* *ship*

Add **ship** or **ness** to these words to make nouns.

relation *good* *sick* *leader* *member* *tidy*

UNIT 2 Revising joins in a word: *ing, ed*

2

Name .... Date ....

Practise the joins. *ing* *ed*

Complete the table.

ed form	**ing** form
	scoring
jumped	
	cheering
danced	
	walking
rolled	

UNIT 3 Revising joins in a word: s

Name ....

Date ....

Practise the joins. ies es ns ps

Complete the table.

ed form	s form
helped	
married	
tackled	
hurried	
stopped	
opened	

UNIT 4 Revising joins in a word: ify

Name ....

Date ....

Practise the joins. ify

Read the definition. Write the word.

Definition	ify word
To make something pure.	p
To make something beautiful.	b
To make something solid.	s
To make something simple.	s
To fill someone with terror.	t
To make something clear.	cl

Name _____   Date _____

Practise the joins.

nn   mm   ss

Pair up and write the words.

tennis
skimmed   bossy
summer   kiss
dinner

holiday
court
boots
milk
time
of life

5

Name _____   Date _____

Practise the joins.

tt   ll   bb

Choose a double letter to finish each word. Write it out.

co __ on _____

li __ le _____

pe __ le _____

bu __ le _____

ba __ oon _____

je __ y _____

bu __ er _____

she __ _____

6

UNIT 7 Revising parallel ascenders and descenders: *pp, ff*

Name

Date

Practise the joins.

pp

ff

Rewrite these words in alphabetical order.

practise here

fast and fluent

suffer

buffet

pepper

supper

cliff

wrapper

traffic

UNIT 8 Revising joins to an anticlockwise letter: *cc, dd*

Name

Date

Practise the joins.

cc

dd

occur

muddy

cappuccino

puddle

adder

accent

Match the definitions to the words.

a kind of snake

frothy coffee

covered in dirt

a way of speaking

a pool of water

to happen

Name _____ Date _____

Practise the letters.

g ____ j ____ x ____ y ____ z ____

Match the definitions to the words.

good to eat with ice-cream _____

this keeps you warm _____

you put things in these _____

like a striped horse _____

colour of the sun _____

type of fruit _____

yellow

jumper   boxes

jelly   orange

zebra

9

Name _____ Date _____

Split the words. Change one part to make a chain.

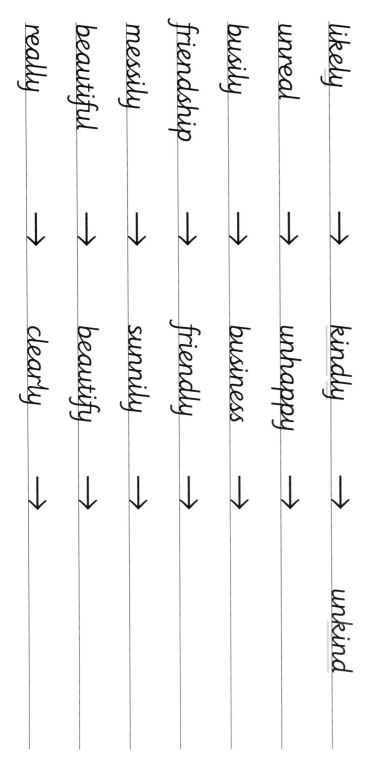

likely → kindly → unkind

unreal → unhappy →

busily → business →

friendship → friendly →

messily → sunnily →

beautiful → beautify →

really → clearly →

10

Name

Date

Copy these funny book titles in sloped writing.

The Arctic Ocean by I.C. Waters

Whodunnit? by Ivor Clew

Winning the Lottery by Jack Potts

Catching Criminals by Hans Upp

Name

Date

Practise the joins.

ad   *af*   *al*

Add **ad**, **af** or **al** to each base word. Write the new word.

al	
though	*most*
mire	*dress*

ad	
fair	*ready*
verb	*front*

af	
vantage	*so*
ford	

Name .... Date ....

Practise the joins.

ight .... *ough* ....

Write rhyming words.

night →	*br*	*sight*	→	*t* ....
bought →	*th*	*flight* →	*fr* ....
tighten →	*t*	*night* →	*f* ....
rough →	*t*	*fought* →	*b* ....

13

Name .... Date ....

Practise the joins.

ious ....

Match the nouns and adjectives.

suspicion ....
infection ....
conscience ....
glory ....
labour ....
seriousness ....

infectious
glorious
laborious
conscious
suspicious
serious

14

15

UNIT 15

Size, proportion and spacing: *able, ful*

Name ....

Date ....

Practise the joins.

able _____   *ful* _____

Make adjectives by adding **able** or **ful**.
Write the whole word.

careful _____

careful _____

fashion _____   *truth* _____   *break* _____

clean _____   *collect* _____   *colour* _____

_____   _____   *help* _____

UNIT 16

Size, proportion and spacing: *fs, ves*

Name ....

Date ....

Practise the joins.

fs _____   *ves* _____

Write the plural of each word.

half _____

shelf _____

loaf _____

sniff _____

wife _____

cliff _____

Name _____   Date _____

Match the words to the abbreviations.

without _____

because _____

hundred _____

different _____

and _____

children _____

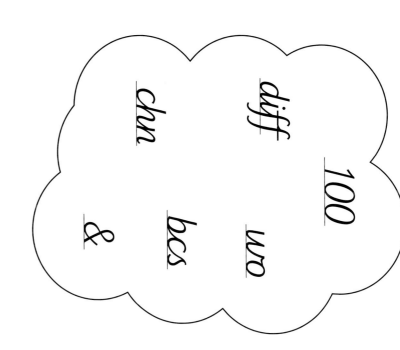

diff

100   wo

chn   bcs

&

17

Name _____   Date _____

Write the most important information in note form.

Trilobites lived about

500 million years ago.

They were the first

creatures with eyes.

They couldn't see very

much because they lived

at the bottom of the sea.

· ·

_____

_____

_____

_____

_____

_____

18

UNIT 19 Speed and fluency: drafting

Name

Date

Write a paragraph about these facts.

Bats

● *sleep upside down*

● *can catch 1,200*
  insects in 1 hour

● *nocturnal mammals*

● *use echo location to*
  find prey

Penpals for Handwriting: Y4

© Gill Budgell (Frattempo) and Kate Ruttle 2009

UNIT 20 Speed and fluency: lists

Name

Date

Sort these things into lists.

Sweet food	**Savoury food**	**Drink**

chocolate *cheese* *jam*

peanuts *water* *milk*

cola *cake* *crisps*

Penpals for Handwriting: Y4

© Gill Budgell (Frattempo) and Kate Ruttle 2009

Name .... Date ....

Practise the joins.

va   vo   ke   ko

Write the words in alphabetical order.

practise here   fast and fluent

van _____

kettle

valley

trick

vowel

track

21

Name .... Date ....

Practise the joins.

ic   ist

Read the definition.
Write the word using **ic** or **ist**.

Definition	Word
(Noun) Someone who cycles.	
(Adj) If you are good at athletics you are …	
(Noun) Someone who does art.	
(Noun) Someone who writes novels.	
(Adj) If you have a lot of energy you are …	
(Noun) Someone who plays the piano.	

22

UNIT 23 Size, proportion and spacing: *ion*

Name _____ Date _____

Practise the joins.

sion   *tion*

Finish the word with **sion** or **tion**. Write the whole word.

crea _____

conclu _____

addi _____

divi _____

exten _____

educa _____

multiplica _____

subtrac _____

UNIT 24 Size, proportion and spacing: *its* and *it's*

Name _____ Date _____

Practise the joins.

its   *it's*

Fill the gaps with **its** or **it's**.

really hot today. I saw a car

go by with _____ roof down. The

dog has been sleeping in _____

basket all day — _____ too hot to

run around, but _____ just the

weather for swimming.

Name _____ Date _____

Practise the joins.

ible   *able*

Add **ible** or **able**. Write the whole word.

imposs _____   improb _____

horr _____   terr _____

enjoy _____   agree _____

25

Name _____ Date _____

Match the words to the meanings.

a baby goose

a taxi

a small kitchen

makes your voice louder

a small tree

a thin book

kitchenette
minicab
microphone
sapling
gosling
booklet

26

27

UNIT 27 Print alphabet: captions, headings, labels

Name

Date

Print these words to label the diagram of the eye.

| pupil | iris | eyelid | eyelash | tearduct |

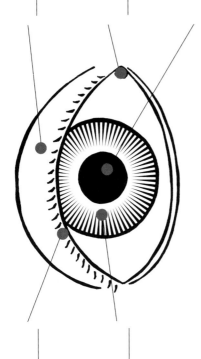

Write a caption.

UNIT 28 Print capitals: posters

Name

Date

Write the words in print capitals on the poster.

SPORTS DAY

WEDNESDAY 21ST JULY

ON THE

PLAYING FIELD

RACES

GAMES

COMPETITIONS

Choose a piece of your own handwriting.

Read the statements and fill in the table.

Practise any joins you need to improve.

	Yes	No
1 The letters are all formed correctly.		
2 The letters all rest on the line except for the descenders, which hang below it.		
3 The small letters are all the same size.		
4 Ascenders and descenders are the same length and are parallel.		
5 Capital letters are not joined. They are the same height as ascenders.		
6 Diagonal joins are all made correctly.		
7 Horizontal joins are all made correctly.		
8 The slope of the writing is even.		
9 The writing was done quickly and smoothly.		
10 The writing is clear, easy to read, and well presented, with print letters used for headings, labels and captions.		

Copy out the joke in a suitable style. Decorate the page too!

Question:

Where do hamsters

come from?

· ·

Answer:

Hamsterdam!

A B C D E F G H I J K L M N O P Q R S T U V W X Y Z

Penpals for Handwriting © Gill Budgell (Frattenpo) and Kate Ruttle 2009

for right-handers

Penpals
writing mat

a b c d e f g h i j k l m n o p q r s t u v w x y z

abcdefghijklmnopqrstuvwxyz

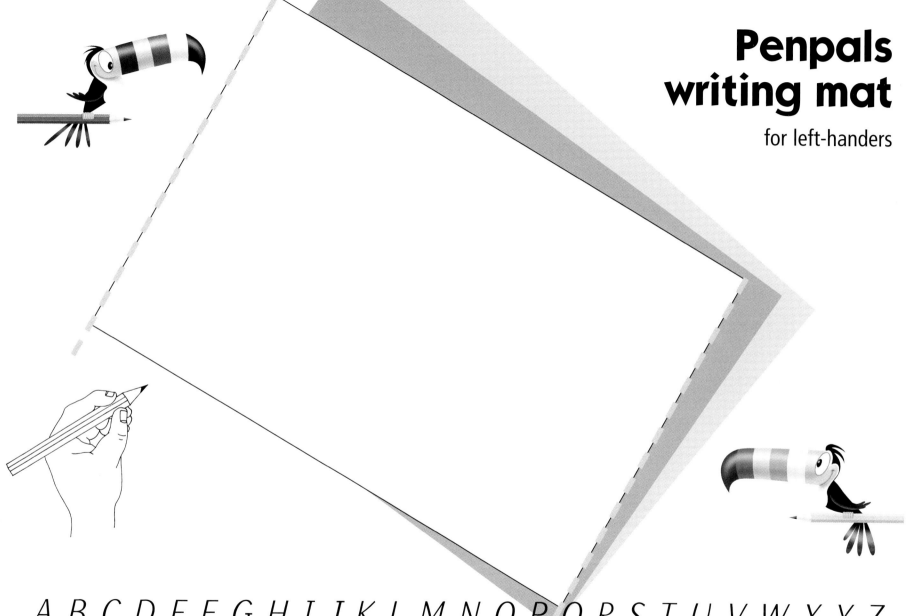

**Penpals
writing mat**

for left-handers

ABCDEFGHIJKLMNOPQRSTUVWXYZ

Practice sheet